MARTIN LUTHER'S

Easter Book

MARTIN LUTHER'S
Easter Book

edited by

ROLAND H. BAINTON

MINNEAPOLIS

MARTIN LUTHER'S EASTER BOOK

Cover Design by Craig P. Claeys
Text Design by Lois Stanfield, LightSource Images

Library of Congress Cataloging-in-Publication Data

Luther, Martin, 1483–1546.
  [Sermons. English. Selections]
  Martin Luther's Easter book / edited by Roland H. Bainton.
      p.   cm.
  Excerpts from the author's sermons.
  Originally published: Philadelphia : Fortress Press, 1983.
  Includes bibliographical references.
  ISBN 0-8066-3578-9 (alk. paper)
    1. Jesus Christ—Passion—Sermons.   2. Jesus Christ—Resurrection—Sermons.
3. Easter—Sermons. 4. Lutheran Church—Sermons.
I. Bainton, Roland Herbert, 1894– . II. Title.
BT431.L87213   1997
252 '.63—dc21   97-28980
                                                                    CIP

The paper used in this publication meets the minimum requirements of American National Standard for Information Sciences—Permanence of Paper for Printed Library Materials, ANSI Z329.48   ∞

Manufactured in the U.S.A.   AF 9-3578

01   00   99   98   97   1   2   3   4   5   6   7   8   9   10

CONTENTS

Introduction

ALTHOUGH LUTHER PREACHED many sermons on the Gospels, we have included excerpts in this book only from sermons related to Jesus' passion and resurrection.

Can the bones of Luther's sermons live again? Not all of them certainly. There are too many. A modern German rendering of Luther's sermons on the Gospels makes five huge volumes of nearly three thousand pages. Besides, some of the bones are vestigial and of interest only to historical specialists. If Luther is to be widely read in our day, he will have to be excerpted. That which is selected must have an element of the universal, yet, if it is completely denuded of its temporal vestments, it will be only naked spirit. Great preaching is that which relates the timeless to time, and it cannot be transferred to another time simply by divesting it of all reference to its own era. For that reason, the effort has been made here to select from Luther's sermons passages that deal not only with man as man but also with man as German. No equivalents have been substituted for the names of coins—*heller, florin,* and *gulden.* References remain to the Reichstag, the Kaiser, and to such places as Wittenberg, Erfurt, and the Joachimstal.

Thus Luther prompts us not to repeat his preaching but to imitate it by doing for our time what he did for his.

We should bear in mind, incidentally, that the problem of translating into the terms of another age applies not only to Luther but to the Gospels themselves. They were written years ago against a Palestinian background of simple, rural communities occupied with sowing, reaping, fishing, tanning, and carrying water from the well. Luther's setting was actually closer to that of the Gospels than is our own.

Take for example two sayings from the Sermon on the Mount—"Ye are the light of the world" and "Ye are the salt of the earth." The first referring to light is universal if light be simply light. At this point there has been no change in a million years. But if we go on and read, "Which of you takes a lamp?" then we are in the age that preceded the incandescent bulb. Again, "Ye are the salt of the earth." Salt as a seasoning is universal, but salt as a preservative has been superseded by refrigeration. If one would convey the full sense of these sayings, whether in the Gospels or in Luther, one has to explain how salt formerly was used!

Luther is removed from us not only by the outward aspects of his culture but even more profoundly by a state of mind. He belonged to the Middle Ages in his envelopment by the supernatural. Heaven then lay close to earth. Angels, saints, and demons hovered over the abodes of men. To whom among us would it ever have occurred, as it did to Luther, that the Virgin Mary, when the boy Jesus was lost, should have reproached herself with the thought that because of her negligence God had taken his Son back to heaven? Yet, he had about him much of the spirit of his own little Hans and Magdalene whose simplicity he envied.

In other respects, however, he broke with the tradition of the Middle Ages and stands therefore nearer to us or rather we to him by reason of his break. He dropped the lush profusion of the legendary and adhered strictly to the text of the Gospels. The age of Gothic drew as heavily from the apocryphal as from the canonical gospels, in which, for example, we are told only that Wise Men came from the East. Nothing is said as to their number or rank. The early church began to make them into kings and to make their number three. Not till the tenth century did the artists give them crowns. The names Balthasar, Caspar, and Melchior cannot be traced back further than the sixth century, and not until the fourteenth was one of them given the features of a Negro. By then the three had become regarded as representatives of three races of humankind, the European, the Asiatic, and the African. Luther discarded all of these accretions for himself, though others might believe them if they liked. The legends of the Virgin Mary were similarly rejected, save for one little detail from the apocryphal gospels that Mary was fourteen years of age when confided to Joseph.

The allegory so dear to the Middle Ages, Luther almost entirely left behind. One could hardly expect him not to see in the Good Samaritan the figure of Christ, but in the case of turning water into wine he did not in medieval fashion equate the water with the Old Testament and the wine with the New, though he did have an allegory of his own in that the water stood for the tribulations and the wine for the joys of marriage.

The typology, which from the days of the early church linked the Old Testament and the New, was not repudiated as such by Luther. He too viewed history as a symphony of redemption in which certain themes recurred with variations from the creation of the world until their resolution in Christ. The suffering of Abel foreshadowed the suffering of Christ. The readiness of Isaac to be sacrificed was a foretaste of the sacrifice of Christ. But the stereo-typed crudities of the illuminated manuscripts and the block books of the late Middle Ages disappeared in Luther. In those works a scene from the Gospels was flanked by two typological anticipations from the Old Testament. Christ going down into the tomb had on either side Joseph being let down into the well and Jonah being swallowed by the whale. The resurrection was flanked by Jonah emerging from the whale but not by Joseph being lift-ed out of the pit. Instead, there was Samson carrying off the gates of the city as Christ broke down the gates of hell. A whole series of such triptychs had become conventional. Luther instead treated the Old Testament stories with a graphic human realism and only in the profundities of human experience discovered the patterns of God's dealings with humankind.

The same treatment was applied to the New Testament. With what poignancy Luther imagined the distress of Mary when her son was lost! The quaint fancy that she thought God might have taken him back to heaven does not obscure for us all the anguish of uncertainty and all the self-recrimination with which she reproached herself. Then the joy that follows pain and the un-fathomable paradox that God must first cast down before he can exalt! When Luther meditates on the love of God, on the utter self-emptying power of God's grace to strike a man dead and make him alive, to rout Satan, swallow death, and confer eternal life, how he makes one tremble for fright and quake for joy!

The following material has been taken entirely from Luther's sermons and lectures on the Gospels. In the selection of the excerpts an eye has been had to the piquant, the poignant, and the profound, and at the same time to the comprehensive, both as to the Gospels and as to Luther's ideas. Certainly all the essential themes of the Evangelists are here. If there is little of the eschatological, it is because Luther's interest did not center here, and there is no treatment of the transfiguration, the Gadarene swine, and the withered fig tree because on these themes Luther was not at his best. His own primary emphases are recurrent: the utter marvel of God's love; the salvation of man solely through divine grace and human faith; the futility of man's endeavor to gain a claim upon God and the sheer wonder of the forgiveness of sins; the insistence that though sins be forgiven, sin does not cease and yet that man should not acquiesce in his imperfection and cease to strive.

Much of Luther's preaching was polemical and here arises a doubt whether such portions should be repeated lest they revive the confessional animosities of the sixteenth century. But if they be left out, we shall miss the measure of the man. He lived in the midst of strife. For twenty-five years he was in imminent danger of the stake and was saved only because the emperor was too busy fighting the French, the Turk, and the pope to come to Germany and enforce the Edict of Worms against Luther. Therefore when he talked about the narrow gate, the little flock, the bearing of the cross, his words had a stark realism, intelligible fully only to those who in our day have felt in their flesh the calamities of this century.

The polemic refers not always to the Church of Rome but also to the radicals in Luther's own circle whose attack shook him even more because completely unexpected. Mention in the following sermons will be found to Carlstadt, whom Luther called a Spiritualist because he regarded the physical and sensory as inappropriate for the communication of the divine, which comes only through the Spirit. For that reason, Carlstadt rejected images and church music and denied any physical presence of Christ in the Lord's Supper. One rejoinder requires a comment. Luther found a confirmation of his view in that at the baptism of Jesus the presence of the Spirit did not suffice to proclaim the Lamb of God, but John had to point to him with his physical finger. Now the Gospel says nothing about the finger. Luther must have had in mind a picture like that of a Grünewald in which John points with a highly elongated finger.

As for Luther on the Lord's Supper, since the subject was so controverted alike with the Catholics and the Spiritualists, Luther had occasion to deal with it frequently and with varying emphases. For that reason it has seemed best to set up the illustrative excerpts in a topical arrangement but to to attach to each its date.

Another figure mentioned is Thomas Müntzer, an inflammatory enthusiast, who summoned the elect to usher in the day of the Lord by the slaughter of the ungodly. Luther believed that the minister should never take the sword in defense of the gospel but only the magistrate in the keeping of the peace. The distinction of the two kingdoms, or administrations—the spiritual and the civil—is a constant theme.

The woodcuts accompanying the text are taken from an epitome of Luther's Bible published by his onetime amanuensis Veit Dietrich in 1562 at Frankfurt with the title *Summaria*. These cuts make a departure in the history of gospel iconography. The artist signed himself "VS," standing for Virgil Solis. He was a resident of Nürnberg, born in 1514, who died in his forty-eighth year in 1562. His output was so vast that some have been tempted to try to advance the date of his death in order to get it all in. The German encyclopedia of artists *(Künstler Lexikon)* says that his best work consisted in his biblical illustrations. These were his finest and his most German production. He is not to be compared with Dürer and Cranach, but he is by no means contemptible in craftsmanship and imagination.

The significance of the cuts lies in the break from the traditional style in the iconography of the Gospels. All of the previous German translations, including Luther's, have for the Gospels only the emblems of the evangelists. Solis pictures the successive events.

How shall we account for this change? One is prompted to suggest that the clue lies in Luther's view that the Word of God is his self-disclosure in Christ. The Scripture is only the manger in which lay the baby Jesus, the Word. That in the Scripture is important which proclaims the Word regardless of the season of the year. Luther did not reject the Christian year, but much of his preaching consisted in the exposition of a biblical book from beginning to end. Of all the Gospels, the chief for him was John and especially the discourses. These do not readily lend themselves to illustration, and yet they were illustrated by Virgil Solis. Even more significant was the way in which Luther treated the biblical characters not as the costumed actors in a pageant, but as persons agonizing and exulting over the mysteries of the faith. Such treatment tended to emancipate the biblical scenes from the liturgical framework and thus opened the path toward the profound individual delineations of biblical characters in the painting of a Rembrandt.

Of very great help in the assembling of these excerpts has been the edition of Luther's sermons on the Gospels in five volumes by Erwin Mülhaupt. He has translated all the Latin sermons into German and has rendered Luther's German into modern high German. I have used this work as a guide to the originals in the Weimar edition on which my translations are based.

After this introduction was in type, I was informed by Professor François Bucher, of the department of Fine Arts at Brown University, that Mâle's observation as to the neglect in art of the public ministry of Jesus in the thirteenth century must be qualified in view of the recent discovery of several Bibles of that period copiously illustrated for the Gospels, though the generalization as to the emphasis still stands. This new material increases the puzzle as to why the printed German Bibles of the fifteenth and early sixteenth centuries should have been so parsimonious of illustration for the Gospels. The radicalism of Virgil Solis with reference to this tradition is not affected, though he would appear to have been reverting unwittingly to an earlier tradition. However, in his illustrating of the Johannine discourses he may have been entirely original. A definitive answer at this point calls for more extensive research in the medieval materials.

The brackets used in the following translations from Luther serve to set off explanatory remarks of the translator and summaries rather than translations of Luther.

ROLAND H. BAINTON

The Journey to Jerusalem and Holy Week

Fire from Heaven

(LUKE 9:51-56)

"LORD, WILT THOU that we command fire to come down from heaven and consume them?" asked the disciples. Oh, you disciples! You think that anyone who does not accept Jesus is going straight to hell, and if he won't give Jesus lodging, you say, "To the devil with you." Observe from this passage that the Holy Spirit has a hard time to cool the intemperate zeal of the godly. Christ said, "Just remember whose children you are, namely, children of the Holy Spirit, a spirit of peace and not dissension." Peter in the Garden forgot that and Christ told him to put up his sword into the scabbard, because this was not the time to fight, but to suffer. The Holy Spirit was silent when Christ was reviled and crucified. We are to be of a meek spirit, for the meek shall inherit the earth. This does not mean that we are to be silent when the truth is assailed. We do not fight the wicked because of their lives, but when they revile the Word, we cannot be silent, but must speak. We are not, however, going to be like James and John, wishing vengeance to descend upon the godless and the tyrants. In that case, we are murderers. If God can suffer them, why cannot we? Christ displayed enough zeal when he cried: "Woe unto thee, Chorazin! woe unto thee, Bethsaida!" He tempered his tone when he added, "I praise thee, Father, Lord of heaven and earth, that thou hast hid these things from the wise and prudent, and revealed them unto babes." So also we should say: "Why should I be so hot? God will have it so." We are to take care not to put in our hand. God does not need our fighting. Here we are to suffer and leave vengeance to the Lord. Otherwise we have a bad spirit.

Peter's Confession

(MATTHEW 16:13-17)

OBSERVE THAT CHRIST did not address Peter alone, but all the apostles, since he said, "Who say ye that I am?" He did not say, "Peter, who do you say that I am?" Christ accepted Peter's answer as the answer of all the apostles and disciples. Otherwise he would have asked them one by one, and from this we may also infer that Christ did not say to Peter alone but to all disciples: "Thou art Peter. . . . And I will give unto thee the keys of the kingdom of heaven." How would it be possible to state more clearly that Peter here is not Peter? For Christ said that he was not flesh and blood but the one to whom the Father in heaven had revealed this. Peter, here, therefore, is not a person in his own right, but only a hearer of the Father making this disclosure. Not Simon Bar-Jona answers here, not flesh and blood, but the hearer of the Father's revelation.

Christ said that on this rock he would build his church. If we take this rock to be the power of the pope, what then follows? It will mean that the church of the apostles was no church at all, because for the span of eighteen years Peter was in Jerusalem and had not seen Rome. This can be clearly proved out of Paul's letter to the Galatians where he says that after his conversion he spent three years in Arabia and then went up to Jerusalem to see Peter, and again fourteen years after that he went up once more to Jerusalem to confer with James and John and Peter. Now, who could be so out of his mind as to say that there was at that time no church in Jerusalem because the power of the Roman Church was not yet established? The church is built not upon the rock taken to be the power of the Roman Church but on the faith that Peter confessed on behalf of the whole church. The universal, catholic church existed for so long prior to the Roman Church.

Peter and the Keys

(MATTHEW 16:18-19)

CHRIST SAYS HERE clearly that he gave the keys to Peter. He does not say two kinds of keys, but the keys which he gives to Peter, as if he would say: "Why do you scramble up to heaven after my keys? Haven't you heard that I left them on earth and gave them to Peter? You won't find them in heaven but in Peter's mouth, where I left them. Peter's mouth is my mouth. His office is my office. His keys are my keys. I have no others; I know of no others. What they bind is bound; what they loose is loosed. If there are other keys in heaven or in hell, I do not care about them, nor about what they bind or loose. You should not care about them either. Let them not lead you astray. Hold to Peter, that is, to *my* keys which bind and loose in heaven and no others." See, this is the proper way to think and speak about the keys. Any other interpretation is forced.

Peter and Tax Collecting

(MATTHEW 17:24-27)

CHRIST CAME TO PETER and said: "What do you think, Simon? From whom do the kings of the earth take toll or tribute? From their sons or from strangers?" Peter said, "From strangers." And Jesus said, "Therefore the children are free." This is a lovely story of Christ's attitude toward the government. First, he let Peter be asked by the tax gatherers for the yearly impost in order to have an opportunity to speak about the two kingdoms, the earthly and the heavenly. Before Peter could give an account, Christ came to him and asked from whom the kings of the earth take tribute. His meaning was: "I know very well, Peter, that we are kings and are sons of kings. I am myself the King of Kings. Therefore, no one has the right to take tribute from us. They should rather pay it to us. How is it then possible, my Peter, that they should levy a tax on you, since you are the son of a king? What do you think? Do they have a right to exact it from you?"

Since Christ put the question in a general way, Peter answered in all simplicity and in general, "Not the sons of the kings, but the strangers pay the tax." Peter did not perceive that by these words Christ meant to call him the son of a king. From this we see how genially Christ walked with his disciples. Here he joked and played with Peter as with a child. Because Peter was without guile, Christ took pleasure in his simplicity.

"Except Ye Become as Little Children"

(MATTHEW 18:1-10)

WHEN THE DISCIPLES were disputing who would be the greatest in the Kingdom, Christ set in their midst a child barely able to toddle, thus to show that the greatest apostles, the pillars of Christendom, should learn from a child that could not speak and should say to him, *"Lieber Herr Doktor."* When you see a child on his father's lap you should take off your hat and say, "Herr Doktor, we should be ashamed of ourselves before you." We must become as little children, because a child does not have in his heart the malice of a prince or a noble. He hears the Lord's Prayer and does

not think of the things that disquiet our hearts. He wants to suck sugar in heaven and dreams with delight of golden apples. He leaves big things to the bigwigs and rides on a hobbyhorse. When he hears of death he thinks of it as sleep. He grows in peace, is fresh and sound. So also we must be young in Christ. If we were to become children, then the pope and I and all men would be of one heart and mind.

"Who Is My Mother? And Who Are My Brethren?"

(MATTHEW 12:48)

[Commenting on this text, Luther makes the point that we are not to obey anyone in disobedience to God.]

OUR BISHOPS, PRINCES, AND PAPISTS themselves confess, and must confess, that we have the word of God, and yet they say it is not valid unless commanded by them and confirmed by a council. But how now does the Christian church come to the point of striking God on the mouth and making him speechless? Saying: "We confess that it is thy Word, but it is only to go into effect when we say so." What do you think God from his judgment seat will say to them? "My dear *Junker*, pope, bishops, and princes, whoever you may be, did you not know that it was my Word?" "Yes," you say. "Very well then, why did you not keep it? Because the Christian church did not command it? Are your churches then to control my word? I thought that when I opened my mouth, man would accept my word as settled; and that if all the world said the contrary, the word should be trodden under foot. How would you like it, if you gave a command to a servant in your house, and he went out and asked the maid or a fellow servant whether he should keep it?"

"Come Unto Me"

(Matthew 11:28)

By these words Christ means to say: "Come to me freely without any merit. You have no need to bring me fastings and other good works. Come only with the faith of the heart. Look upon me as a good and gracious Savior. There is no need for anything else. Simply come; I will quicken you. This is no make-believe. I will make your heart and your spirit bold against hell, sin, death, and devil. You will feel it. Now you have a bad conscience; you are depressed, crushed, miserable, poor, anxious, and worried, and there is no one who can give you counsel, comfort, and help. God's wrath against sin is so tremendous. Before his righteousness heaven and earth must bow and no one can be justified before him save through me. Come then to me. Confess your life to be pitiably bad. Such pupils are just the ones I want. This is the sort I invite. I have nothing to do with the well. My Kingdom is a hospital for the sick because I am a doctor. The right kind of patient in my hospital is the one who knows he is sick, who feels the pressure of sin, and who earnestly seeks from me health and comfort and believes that I shall help him. This is the one whom I will make joyful, and I will make him alive, that he shall nevermore die. Therefore, if anyone wishes health, a peaceful conscience, and a quiet heart, let him not run here and there, but come unto me."

Again Christ says, "Take my yoke upon you." That is why 'men do not run to Christ. He puts a yoke on the old donkey. That means a cross. He lays a heavy burden on the neck. But Christ says: "Do not be downcast on this account. Take my yoke upon you; I will help you out of trouble. Let this be enough that I take from your soul the weight and the work and the bad conscience. Be patient if I flay the old ass. He must be killed if I am to make you alive. This is the nature of my Kingdom that those who would come in must constantly die to the desires of the old Adam and be renewed in the spirit through increase in faith."

"Where Two or Three Are Gathered Together"
(MATTHEW 18:18-20)

WHEN I AM TROUBLED AND SAD, distressed and discouraged, no matter what time of day—for public preaching does not go on all the time in the churches—if then my neighbor or brother comes to me, I should unburden myself to him in the assurance that his word of comfort has God's "yes" in heaven. By the same token I am to comfort another and say: "Dear friend, dear brother, why not stop worrying? It is not God's will that sorrow should so afflict you. He has not sent his son to die for you that you should be downcast, but that you should be of good cheer; so then, be joyous and consoled. In that way you will do God a service and please him." Then we should kneel down and say the Lord's Prayer together. It will certainly be heard in heaven, for Christ said, "I am in your midst." He did not say, "I see it; I hear it; and I shall come to you," but he said, "I am already there." When, then, you comfort me and I comfort you and both of us do it to our mutual improvement and blessing, then I should believe you and you should believe me that God, the Heavenly Father, will give us what we ask and what we lack.

Zacchaeus

(LUKE 19:1-10)

ZACCHAEUS DID NOT WANT Christ to enter his house and yet he did. That he did not is plain because he climbed a tree to see Christ go by and did not dare to invite him because he did not consider himself to be worthy. He would be satisfied with a look and to remain unrecognized. But that he really did want him to come is evident from this—that he received him with joy, for joy is the sign of a previous love and desire. If anyone had asked him whether he wanted Christ to come, he would have answered,

"I do not dare to ask or to wish." Here one sees the depths of the human heart whose truth is so deep and whose desire is so hidden that it does not know itself nor rejoice in its own desire.

Jerusalem Beleaguered

(LUKE 21:20)

I AM OPPOSED to the fortification of Wittenberg. The advice that the Lord gave the disciples is best, "When you see Jerusalem compassed with armies . . . , flee." That is what they did. Whether we win or lose, we are done for. I will not be safe when unmarried soldiers have their way. When they come, we shall have to preach what they say or else they will give us nothing to eat. They will glut their lust with matron and maid. Kitchens and cellars must be opened to them. Even the princes will not fare any better. That is why I would not like to be here. I would rather await the end at the hands of the enemy, than so to be protected. Look at what happened in Vienna in peacetime from the soldiers there to defend the city against Turks, and they behaved worse than the Turks. You cannot keep an army in a sack. That is why I am not in favor of the fortification and the garrisoning of Wittenberg. Christ told his disciples to flee, and that is what I say. If we knew the time of our visitation, we should have peace, but instead we drive out the preachers. Because we will not use the light of day, we shall see the night ablaze. And if the walls were as high as heaven and the iron as thick as church walls, still I would not stay because they will do no good. If Christ, the Prince of Peace, is absent, even though the enemy without should do nothing, the city will be worse off than on the outside.

Where will our souls be when all the world is consumed with fire? Tell me, my dear friend, where are you when you are asleep and do not know what is going on outside in the body? Do you think that God is not able to hold the souls in his hand? Do you think he has to have a sheepfold for souls, like a shepherd? It is enough for you to know that souls are in the hands of God. Do not be disturbed because you do not understand how. The master said, "Father, into thy hands, I commend my spirit." Hold to that.

Mary and Martha

(Luke 10:38-42)

LET US FIRST TAKE THIS as simply as it is told, for this is the greatest art—to abide by the simple understanding. The story is that Jesus came to a dwelling and although many people lived there, only Martha took him in. Now Martha had a sister, Mary. They divided the work. Martha went to prepare the food, carry the water, and wash the dishes. Now the Gospel says that this time Martha was doing all of this work alone. Christ had another work to do. He sat and preached and while Mary sat at his feet he took no heed of what Martha was doing. She came and complained, asking the Master to tell Mary to help her. "Look here," she said, "I have given myself so much trouble. I have washed up and put everything straight. Did I not have the right idea?" But God does not care about our idea. Jesus chided her not because of her work but because of her worry. "Martha, Martha," he said, "you are troubled about many things and only one thing is needful." As if he would say: "You are full of care and I have preached that we should have no care; and besides, when the Word is declared, other things should stop. Even more, we should forsake wife, child, father, mother, friends, and foe, honor, and goods, and cling only to the Word." You see, Martha had good intentions, yet he chided her; but he did it gently, and that is what is so fine about the Gospel. God is pictured as a kind, friendly man who deals tenderly with us when we do not do as we ought.

Palm Sunday

(Matthew 21:1-9)

> *"Behold, thy King cometh unto thee, meek,*
> *and sitting upon an ass."*

Look at Christ. He rides not upon a horse which is a steed of war. He comes not with appalling pomp and power but sits upon an ass, which is a gentle beast to bear burdens and to work for men. From this we see that Christ comes not to terrify, to drive, and oppress, but to help and to take for himself our load. We read further that he came from the Mountain of Olives. Now the oil of the olive was the symbol of that which soothes. His entry was marked not by the clash of weapons and the cries of war, but by singing, praise, rejoicing, and the blessing of God.

"Thy King cometh unto thee."

Observe that he comes. You do not seek him; he seeks you. You do not find him; he finds you. The preachers come from him, not from you, and their preaching comes from him and not from you. Your faith comes, not from you, but from him.

He is lowly. This brings us from faith to the example of love. Christ gives you faith with all its benefits, and you are to give your neighbor love with all its benefits. You may then ask what are the good works that you should do for your neighbor? They have no name. Just as the good works which Christ has done for you have no name, so the good works which you do for your neighbor have no name. How, then, are they to be recognized? Answer: they have no name for this reason, lest they be divided and this done and that left undone. Rather you must give yourself to your neighbor utterly, just as Christ did not confine himself to prayer and fasting for you. These are not the works which he did for you, but he gave himself completely not only with prayer and fasting, with all works and suffering, so that there was nothing in him that was not made yours and done for you. So this is not your good work, that you should give alms or pray, but rather that you should give yourself entirely to your neighbor, as he needs and as you can, with alms, prayer, fasting, counsel, comfort, teaching, appeal, reproof, pardon, clothes, food, and also suffering and death on his behalf. But tell me, where in all Christendom are such works?

Would that I had a voice of thunder to resound throughout the world against that expression "good works," that it might be rooted out of heart, mind, ears, and books, or else correctly understood. A good work is called "good" because it is helpful and does good to him to whom it is done. What good is it to wear a costly robe or build a lordly mansion? What good is it to adorn churches with silver and gold and statues of stone or wood? What good if every hamlet had ten bells as big as those of Erfurt?

The Cleansing of the Temple

(JOHN 2:13-16)

IN JOHN'S GOSPEL the cleansing of the Temple appears to come directly after the Baptism of Christ, whereas in Matthew's Gospel it comes after the entry into Jerusalem on Palm Sunday. It is not important to settle this question. It may be that John has jumped over the entire interval from the beginning of Jesus' ministry to the last Passover because less interested in the deeds than in the words of Christ. Be that as it may. If you cannot contrive a reconciliation of John and Matthew, let it go. You won't be damned on that account.

The cleansing of the Temple presents a graver problem in that Christ, who was only a private person and not a civil ruler, behaved like a ruler. The prophet said that Messiah should smite the earth with a rod of his mouth (Isaiah 11:4). This means that

Christ should not have the sword in the hand because there it belongs to the magistrate. Rather, Christ's sword should be that which proceeds from the mouth, and the sword of the mouth is nothing other than the Word of God. But in that case, if the Kingdom of Christ is restricted to the sword of the mouth, why did Christ use the sword of the fist? I think it was a concession to the Old Testament just as when Christ allowed himself to be circumcised. Sometimes he followed Moses and sometimes he rejected him. Sometimes he kept and sometimes broke the Sabbath. But in the New Testament the two jurisdictions are sharply distinguished. I, as a minister, have a spiritual rod in the mouth; you, as a magistrate, a physical rod in the fist. I am not to tell you how to punish and strike, nor are you to tell me how to preach. That would be overstepping your bounds.

"Let Not Your Heart Be Troubled"

(JOHN 14:1-14)

HERE YOU ARE to see how warm, faithful, and friendly was the Lord Jesus to his disciples that he left them not without comfort on the very night he was to be taken from them through his bitter suffering and cross, and would leave them behind in danger, fear, and terror. While he had been with them, they were full of assurance. Now he let them know it would be different. Their hearts would be full of fright and dismay, as indeed it happened when he was so shamefully and cruelly done to death. This was not the Christ who had raised the dead and cleansed the Temple. Now he was weak and trampled under foot. Then the hearts of the disciples were congealed with fear and they dared nothing, but cried in anguish: "Oh, where shall we stay? He has been our comfort and defense, and now he is gone. There is no one now to protect us. Our enemies are strong and mighty, and we are abandoned by the world." That is why Christ spoke these words, to show them in advance the coming terror and to comfort them that they might remember and be upheld.

If then you would be a Christian like the apostles and the saints, arm yourselves, and be certain that someday an hour will come when your heart will be terrified and shaken. This is said to all Christians to make them realize that their present security will not last long. Today is tranquil; tomorrow will be different. The devil can strike a javelin into the heart, or some other distress will overtake you. See to it then that you are armed and take comfort from God's Word.

From this assurance we must learn and know what Christ is like. He is not one to strike terror and sorrow because he has come to take away terror and sorrow and to give instead a light heart and a free conscience. That is why he promised to send to his disciples the Holy Spirit, the Comforter. The Christian, then, may be subject outwardly to much suffering and distress, but at the same time can be comforted and joyful in heart and mind toward God. Let us learn that whatever misfortune may overtake us, be it pestilence, war, high prices, poverty, persecution, or dismal imaginations which smite the head and crush the heart, we may conclude that all of this is from Christ to guard us against the devil who can disguise himself with the very form and name of Christ.

"Ye Believe in God, Believe Also in Me"

(JOHN 14:1)

UP UNTIL NOW it has been said that the Holy Spirit rules the councils, determines the articles of faith, and confers papal decrees. This is the greatest dishonor that one can do to the Holy Spirit. This is to make the Holy Spirit into a dead law rather than a living principle written by the Spirit in the heart. The Holy Spirit comes down from heaven, fills men, and makes their tongues as flames of fire that they may fear nought.

Temples of God

(JOHN 14:23)

IT IS A GREAT CONSOLATION that he will make his abode with us. Where God is, there is his temple. God's abode is where he speaks, works, and is found. This occurs in a true Christian man, and nothing is more precious. What is it to have temples of gold? We are enraged if the Turk destroys temples and altars, but in the meantime we destroy the true temples of God. We seek to defend with the sword temples of wood built by man and destroy man, the temple built by God.

"God So Loved the World"

(JOHN 3:16)

THESE ARE ASTOUNDING WORDS. God has every reason to be angry and to wipe out the world as a frightful enemy, and yet there is no greater lover than God and no more desperate scoundrel than the world. To love the world and wish it well is beyond me. If I were God, I would give it hellfire. But instead of consuming the world in anger, God loves the world with such unspeakable and overflowing love that he gave his Son. My powers are not adequate to reach to the bottom of this tremendous affirmation. This love is greater than the fire seen by Moses [in the burning bush], greater even than the fire of hell. Who will despair if God so loves the world?

> *"That he gave his only-begotten son, that whosoever believeth in him should not perish, but have eternal life."*

The words read so simply but are so mighty. They are greater than the heavens and the sun. God will give us eternal life. If he offered us a dukedom or a kingdom, we should dispute and say: "It cannot be. He would not give me a kingdom." We think we are not worth more than twenty gulden, for what is man compared with God? But see now what God has in mind, that he should not strangle, terrify, and harass mankind, but rather should give life, even eternal life. Compare life with every other gift on earth. Would one give his life for the kingdom of France? Hardly, nor even for the whole world. But now God is going to give life which is better than all the treasures of the world, and not only life but eternal life. What is the reason? It is that God so loved the world. These are overwhelming words.

God's gifts are inexpressible. What does he give? His only begotten Son. This is not the gift of a groshen, an eye, a horse, a cow, or a kingdom. No, nor heaven with the sun and the stars, nor the whole creation, but his Son, who is as great as himself.

This should kindle sheer light, yes, fire, in our hearts, that we should ever dance for joy. If God gives his Son, he withholds nothing, for he gives himself.

"All things are yours," as Paul says, "whether Paul or Apollos or Cephas, or the world, or life, or death, or things present, or things to come; all are yours; and ye are Christ's; and Christ is God's" (1 Corinthians 3:21-23).

This treasure is not given as a reward. It is a gift. It is your own. You have only to accept it. It is not a castle, but God's Son who is given. Hold out your hand and take, but the world is so possessed of the devil as to be unwilling to be simply a receiver. God certainly has to be a great forgiver in order to forgive the world, which so reviles him. When, then, God gives so much to the world, gives indeed his very self, how can the world hate him? Think of what I have done myself! For fifteen years I said Mass, crucified Christ, and practiced idolatry in the cloister, and yet God sent his Son for me and forgave me everything. O Lord God, ought we not to rejoice and not only serve gladly but suffer and laugh at death for the sake of him who has given us such a treasure? If I believe this, should I not be willing to be burned at the stake?

"My Peace I Give Unto You"

(JOHN 14:27)

WHEN YOU ARE in the midst of suffering Christ says: "I will make you feel as if you were in paradise. In war I will give you peace; in death, life."

"When the Comforter Comes"

(JOHN 15:26)

THAT WE FAIL NOT, Christ said, "I will send you a Comforter."
When my sins and the fear of death affright me, then he comes
and touches my heart and says: "For shame! Up again!" He
breathes upon us a new spirit and speaks to us in a friendly and
comforting way, that we should not quail before death even if we
had ten necks but rather should say, "Even though I have sinned,
I have come through and had I still enough sins to engulf me I
would yet hope not to be hurt." This is not to say, of course, that
we should not feel our sins, for the flesh must feel them, but the
Spirit overcomes them and cows fear and despair. What then can
the creature do against us if the Creator be for us?

All Shall Bear Witness

(JOHN 15:27)

IT IS NOT ENOUGH that we believe. We must also testify, and yet
recognize that to do so lies beyond our power. The Lord gives the
reason when he says, "They will put you under the ban" (John
16:2). If you wish to witness and say very much about Christ, you
will have an adversary. Lucifer and his angels will swoop upon you
like a thousand wolves about a sheep. When the devil sees you
lighting a lamp to enlighten others he begins to rage. He can
stand it better if you believe only for yourself. But if you want
to kindle a light for others, you will be in danger of death, as
we see by experience. This fulfills the word of Christ. "The time

cometh, that whosoever killeth you will think he doeth God's service" (John 16:2).

Asking the Father

(JOHN 16:23)

THIS IS AN EXHORTATION to prayer in extreme anxiety. Certain it is that when there is no distress there is no prayer. Or if there is a prayer it is feeble and listless, without sap and drive. That is why troubles are so needful. It is better to suffer a trial than to own a house, for all the riches in the world are not to be compared with a severe trial. The reason is that when there is no trial we are complacent and do not ask nor seek after God, but when distress overtakes us we have two kinds of prayer. The first cannot be expressed, as when Paul spoke of "groanings unutterable" (Romans 8:26). This prayer never ceases, and no one sees it save the one who makes it and even he does not know how deep it is. For example, when someone lies in prison for the gospel and is to be burned, he prays and prays so mightily that he himself has never known such powerful prayer. No one by tongue or pen can make a prayer as strong as this. Then comes the second kind of prayer, the outward, as when he who opens to a psalm derives comfort from it. What a relish he has for it! One sees in the heart of such a man pure humility and compassion for his enemies.

The Lord then will comfort those who make such prayers. No one can pray who has not known calamity. Prayers are unavailing which lack the great treasure, the holy cross.

"I Know My Sheep"

(JOHN 10:1–18)

WE SHOULD BE COMFORTED that he calls us sheep. One person may lack gold, goods, health, another something else. It seems, then, as if we were in the jaws of the wolf and had no shepherd. By no means does it appear as if Christ so loved us. We see and feel quite otherwise in life and death, but we must hear his whistle and learn to know him. "I am your shepherd; you are my sheep because you hear my voice. In this way you know me, and I know you." This knowledge is through faith.

The Lord's Supper

An Outward Sign

[1520]

QUITE COMMONLY GOD has given along with the Word a sign as a further assurance and strengthening of faith. Noah was given the sign of the rainbow, Abraham of circumcision, Gideon of the dew upon the fleece. This happens when men make a will. There is not only a word but also a notary's seal to show that it is valid and trustworthy, and so Christ in making his testament attached a seal and sign to the words, namely his own true flesh and blood under the bread and wine.

Not an Untouchable Charm

[1522]

A CHRISTIAN SHOULD KNOW that there is on earth no greater holiness than God's Word. The Sacrament itself is made blessed and hallowed through God's Word by which we are all spiritually born and consecrated to Christ. If then a Christian with mouth,

ears, heart, and the whole body may lay hold of the Word which hallows all things and is above the sacraments, why may he not touch that which is hallowed through the Word? Otherwise he should not so much as touch his own body, because he is himself as hallowed as the Sacrament. A Christian is holy in body and soul, whether layman or priest, man or woman. To say the contrary is to blaspheme Holy Baptism, the blood of Christ, and the grace of the Holy Spirit. A Christian is great and rare, and God cares more about him than about the Sacrament, for the Christian is not made for the Sacrament, but the Sacrament for the Christian, and these blind heads want to dispute whether the Sacrament may be touched, and make a heresy out of so doing. Away with these hardened and infatuated heathen who do not know what a Christian is! God deliver us from them.

Inward and Unconstrained

[1522]

[Over against the position of the Roman Catholics, Luther constantly stressed the inwardness of the Sacrament.]

THE OUTWARD AND THE INWARD partaking of the Sacrament are to be carefully distinguished. To take the elements is outward and that can be done without faith and love. If such reception made a Christian, then a mouse would be a Christian, for a mouse can nibble the bread and even sip the wine. The inner, spiritual, true reception is quite something else and consists in the use and the fruit, which take place in faith.

But not all people have this faith. For that reason no ordinance should be made out of this Sacrament like the silly requirement of the holy father, the pope, that everyone go to Mass at Easter on pain of being denied Christian burial. Is not that a foolish command? We are not all alike and do not have all the same faith. One has a stronger faith than another. For that reason there can be no general ordinance. It is because of this that at Easter the greatest sins are committed by unworthy participation, all on account of this unchristian command which seeks to drive and force people to the Sacrament. And why? Because the pope cannot see into the heart, whether faith be there or not. If you believe that God takes your part and gives his blood for you, if you believe that God says: "Follow me unaffrighted. Let us see what can harm you. Let the devil, death, sin, hell, and all creatures do their worst. If I am for you, if I am your guard and protector, trust me and follow boldly after me"—he who believes this belongs here and takes the Sacrament as an assurance, seal, or pardon, that he is certain of the divine assurance and promise. But such faith we do not all have. Would to God that one-tenth of the people had it!

Everyone cannot have such a rich, overflowing treasure, with which out of grace we are showered by God. They alone possess it who have endured physical or spiritual torments in the body through persecution or in the spirit through a devastating conscience. When the devil outwardly or inwardly makes the heart weak, fearful, and crushed, so that it does not know how it stands with God, and sin looms before it, then in such a stricken heart God will dwell, for who needs a protector and guard if he has not gone through torment and his sins gnaw daily? In that case he does not belong at this table because this food calls for hungry and questing spirits. He who does not feel this should abstain for a time from the Sacrament because this food will not enter a satisfied and full heart, but if we sense qualms of conscience and the foreboding of a heart dismayed, then we shall come with all humility and reverence, not tripping and trotting. But we are not always in the mood. Today I have grace and I am ready, but tomorrow, no. Perhaps six months from now I shall have no desire or readiness. They are best prepared who are always beset by death and the devil. They are the very ones who are most likely to have the faith that nothing can harm them, because they have in themselves that which no one can take away. That is why, when Christ instituted the Sacrament, he first dismayed his disciples when he told them that he would go away from them, and he cut them deeply when he said that one of them would betray him. Do you not think that these words went to their very hearts? They must have been appalled and sat there as if everyone of them had betrayed God, and only when Christ saw them tremble, quake, and quail did he institute the Holy Sacrament to their comfort. Wherefore, the bread is a consolation to the troubled and medicine for the sick, life for the dying, food for the hungry, and a rich treasure for the poor and needy.

Sufficient for today on the use of the Sacrament, I commend you to God.

Also Outward

[1525]

NO ONE CAN DENY that the three Evangelists, Matthew, Mark, and Luke, and also Paul, say that Christ took the bread and blessed it and broke it and gave it to his disciples saying, "Take eat, this is my body which is broken for you." And again the cup, saying, "This is my blood of the new covenant." Then in addition to these four powerful passages there is another in 1 Corinthians 10:16: "The cup of blessing, which we bless, is it not a communion of the blood of Christ? The bread which we break, is it not a communion of Christ?" There's a thunderclap for Dr. Carlstadt. Do you hear this, my dear brother? The bread broken and distributed in pieces is a communion of the body of Christ. It is, it is, it is, says Paul, a communion of the body of Christ. But what is the communion of the body of Christ? It could not be anything other than that those who take the broken bread, each one a piece, receive in it the body of Christ. This communion means to participate in the body of Christ, so that each one with the other receives the common body of Christ. Paul says that we are all one body, and we all partake of one bread. That is why it has long been called the Communion, that is, a fellowship.

Here Dr. Carlstadt performs gymnastics to get away from the sense of this text. He employs his perverted trick of interpreting only in a spiritual and inward sense that which God has instituted physically and outwardly, and, on the other hand, of making outward and physical that which God has made inward and spiritual. He takes the word "communion" and says this means only spiritual communion, so that the communion of the body of Christ means that we reflect upon and share his suffering.

But communion with the suffering of Christ cannot be a communion with the flesh and blood of Christ because anyone who would suffer with Christ or participate in his sufferings must be godly, spiritual, and believing. A sinful, fleshly man could not do that, but even the unworthy can partake in the body of Christ, as Paul says (1 Corinthians 11:29), "He that eateth and drinketh unworthily, eateth and drinketh damnation to himself." That is what happened to Judas. With all the other disciples at the Last Supper, he partook of the body and the blood of Christ. He received it and ate and drank just as much as the others.

My dear friend, the natural meaning of language is an empress, and goes far beyond any subtle, hair-splitting, sophisticated interpretation. One must not depart from the natural sense unless an obvious article of faith compel it, otherwise no letter of the Scripture will be safe from these crystal-gazers.

Christ's Body Not in Heaven

[1527]

BUT WE ARE TOLD that Christ is not bodily in the Sacrament because he ascended into heaven and sits at the right of God. When we read this we are not to think of a cardboard heaven such as children like to color and put in it a golden chair with Christ sitting beside the Father wearing a chorister's cape or a golden crown. If it were not for such pictures, there would not be so much dispute nor such insistence that Christ must be in a particular locality. The right hand of God is not a place, because God is essentially present in all the ends of the earth, in and through all creatures. We know that God's arm, hand, face, spirit, and wisdom are all the same thing. We know that the whole godhead dwells bodily in Christ (Colossians 2:9). How, then, can it also be true that in the cradle, in the Temple, in the wilderness, in the town and villages and gardens and fields, on the cross, in the grave—and at the same time in heaven in the bosom of the Father? If, now, according to our faith, it is true that the godhead was essentially and personally present in Christ on earth in so many places, and at the same time in heaven and with the Father, then we must conclude that the godhead is everywhere present and essentially and personally fills heaven and earth and everything with his nature and majesty, as Jeremiah says (Jeremiah 23:23-24), "I fill heaven and earth and am a God who is near," and the Psalmist says (Psalm 139:7), "Who can flee from his presence?"

For this reason, if Christ had never spoken the words at the Lord's Supper, "This is my body," nevertheless the saying that

Christ sits at the right hand of God shows that his body and blood can be there and also in all other places at the same time. There is no need here for any transubtantiation or any transformation of the bread into his body. He can be there without all this because the right hand of God does not first have to be changed into all things in which it is present. We are not so crude as to suppose that Christ's body is in the bread in so crass and visible a manner as bread is in a basket or wine is in a jar, as the Radicals claim we do. We believe that his body is there, as the words say: "This is my body." We do not care about the expression. We are ready to say he is in the bread, he is where the bread is, or as you will. We will not quarrel about words so long as this remains—that this is not ordinary bread which we eat in the Lord's Supper, but it is the body of Christ.

Why not, then, eat the body of Christ anywhere because he is everywhere present? Because you are not to try to eat him as you would sauerkraut and soup on your table, but only where he wishes. He is not to be seized, and you will not lay hold of him, even if he is in your bread, unless he binds himself to you and brings himself through his word to the particular table, that you partake of him there.

Do Not Worry or Pry into the Inscrutable

[1534]

CHRISTIANS SHOULD DO GOD HONOR and believe that God can do what he says. They should not be like the Radicals who trouble themselves to know how bread can be body and wine can be blood. They want to comprehend God, and because this does not agree with reason, they assume that God cannot do it; but why should man torment himself to death to make everything agree with reason? If it is God's Word, he is almighty and true. Then, we should accept in faith, simply, like children. We should be thankful and joyous and ask for what purpose he has done it—not whether he can. There is no man among us who knows how the eye sees, how we go to sleep, and how we wake up. The voice of the preacher fills several thousand ears and hearts. I see it and hear it but do not understand it. We want to be masters and judges in matters which are hidden from us, and we do not understand our daily lives. What happens that the tongue moves in the mouth to make speech? No man can tell you how a hair grows. If then, we cannot grasp that in which we live and move, how shall we comprehend that which God alone discloses and in which we do not live? You can judge that your cow eats hay and grass. Gold, silver, stone, and corn—all this reason can handle—but what God does with the tongue, the eyes, and the ears, you will have to leave undisputed. The thing for you to ask is whether God or man has spoken and whether it is a work of God or man. If it is God's Word and work, then shut your eyes and do not ask how it happens. I should be baptized and become pure from all my sins. That is his Word. So also here: come, eat, "do this in remembrance of me." This is his true flesh and blood because his Word says so, and not that of a man. He has instituted it and commanded it. Baptism in his sacrament and work. I feel and hear well enough what he says, but what takes place I do not know. Do not give yourself over, then, to questions and disputes, but consider the use and the joy of the Sacrament.

He has made it as easy and as lovable as possible. Whether you stand or sit does not matter. He has laid no hard work upon us. Eating and drinking is the easiest thing. There is nothing men would rather do. It is the most joyous exercise on earth. As the proverb says, "No dancing before eating," or again, "A happy head crowns a full stomach." He invites you to a sweet friendly meal and will lay no heavy burden upon you. There is nothing about cowls, nothing about pilgrimages in armor to Jerusalem, circumcision, sacrifices of animals, and ablutions as in the law, but he says: "You have the Lord's Supper. When you come together and would learn of me, take bread and wine and repeat the words, 'This is my body and blood.'"

[1519]

FROM ALL THIS it is clear that the Sacrament is nothing other than a divine sign whereby Christ and all saints with all their works, sufferings, merits, graces, and goods are given as consolation and strength to all who are sore beset by the devil, sin, the world, the flesh, and all evil. To receive the Sacrament is to believe this, for everything depends on faith. It is not enough to know what the Sacrament is and means. You must believe that you have received it. There are those who puzzle themselves as to how the whole of Christ's body and blood can be present in such a tiny piece of bread and sip of wine. You do not need to be concerned about that. It is enough if you know that this is a divine sign and that Christ's flesh and blood are truly here. How and where they are present you may leave to him. When you are downcast be assured that in this Sacrament, Christ and all saints come to you with all their virtues, suffering, and grace. They live, suffer, and die with you and seek to be wholly yours and to share in all things with you. If you will exercise and increase this faith, you will experience what a joyous marriage feast your God has prepared for you upon the altar.

Let the Unexamined Abstain

[1523]
THIS YEAR, ONCE MORE, we shall allow each to come to the Sacrament according to his own judgment, but in the future no one will be admitted who has not first been examined and declared how his heart stands, whether he knows what the Sacrament is, and why he comes.

But the Timorous Are Invited

[1528]
NOW THAT WE HAVE a proper understanding and doctrine of the Sacrament, a word of exhortation is in order that this great treasure, which is daily dispensed among Christians, should not be neglected. Those who are Christians should dispose themselves to partake often. There are a great many who, now that we are freed from the pope, will go for one, two, or three years and even longer without the Sacrament, as if they were such strong Christians that they did not need it. Some, again, are deterred because we have

taught that they only should come who are driven by hunger and thirst. Some even say that it is free and not necessary and it is enough if one believes. The greater part are callous and despise alike God's Word and the Sacrament. Now it is true that we said none should be compelled and the Sacrament should not be made into soul torture. At the same time these folk should recognize that those who for so long a time abstain are not to be regarded as Christians, for Christ did not institute the Lord's Supper as a spectacle to be gazed upon, but as a supper to eat, drink, and remember.

I know from experience, and anyone can find it out for himself, that if one does stay away from day to day, one will grow more callous and cold and in the end will be carried away by the wind. One should examine the heart and conscience and see whether one is of those who desire to be right with God. The more that happens, the more will the heart be warm and kindled.

[1529]

BUT YOU SAY, "I am not worthy." Well, that is my temptation too. You heard in the papists' sermons that we should be entirely pure, without a blemish. That is why we are so timorous, and the heart at once says, "I am not worthy"; so I decide to wait until the next Sunday, until I am better; and the next Sunday goes over to the next, and so on till the quarter of the year, and the half, and the whole. But if I waited until I were entirely pure and had no more reproaches of conscience, I should in that case never come, or not for a very long time.

A distinction is to be made, however, in the case of brazen sinners guilty of adultery, usury, extortion, theft, public hate, or envy. To such rough, wild persons one should say, "Stay away." They are not ready for the forgiveness of sins. They wish to remain evil.

But if your sins are not such that they should be publicly reproved by the congregation, you should not abstain, but should say to yourself: "I do not come in my own righteousness. In that case I would never come. A child is not baptized because it is godly, and I do not go to confession because I am pure. I go as one who is unworthy, who cannot be worthy. God preserve me from being unworthy." We are always looking at our hands rather than at Christ's mouth. We ought to say, "I see what thou sayest, not what I do."

[1534]

STRANGE THAT SOME ARE AFRAID of the Sacrament! The peasants are troubled because they think they must have left all their sins. No wonder that under the papacy the people took it so hard! The papists have corrupted the Sacrament with gall, vinegar, and wormwood, and taken all the joy out of it, for we were taught that we must be so pure that not one fleck of the least sin should remain upon us, and so holy that for sheer holiness our Lord God could not look upon us. I was not able to find that in myself, and on that account I was terrified and I am still plagued by this residue from the papacy, but now joy is coming back. Of course, it is true that we should be godly, and if you love your sins more than God's grace, stay away. But the Lord's Supper is a sweet, savory food, from which you are not to derive poison and death. Listen, it is given for you, not against you. For your soul's comfort, strength, and redemption was it given. Christ does not put you under the water of baptism in order to drown you, but that you may be saved from your sins and likewise in the Lord's Supper. That is why you should learn the use and the purpose. Here Christ has established the Sacrament for you and for me. I feel that I am a scoundrel, that the devil has taken hold of me, that I do not do what I should. People in this case ought to be invited to take the Sacrament. They should not dread it as a frightful judgment. That feeling arises from the old custom or from the devil, but Christians should come with joy and confidence and think: "I will eat his flesh and blood. Why has he given them to me? Surely he will not cast me off if I seek only in his name to be blessed and look for help and comfort."

The Sacrament of Love

[1522]

YESTERDAY WE HEARD about the true use of the Holy Sacrament. Now we come to the fruit of this Sacrament, namely, love, that we may behave toward our neighbor as God toward us. From God we have received nothing but love and kindness, for Christ has given his all for us, which no angel can comprehend, for God is a glowing bake oven full of love that reaches from earth to heaven. Love, I say, is the fruit of this Sacrament, but as yet I see little of it here at Wittenberg, though there has been much preaching about it. Love is the greatest, but nobody attends to it above all else, but rather to that which does not matter. Paul says, "If I speak with the tongues of men and of angels, and have not love, I am become a sounding brass and a tinkling cymbal." Those are terrifying words of Paul's. "And if I have all wisdom and all knowledge to understand God's secrets, if I have faith so as to move mountains and have not love, it is nothing. And if I give my goods to feed the poor and my body to be burned, and have not love, it profiteth nothing." There is nobody here who has given all his goods to feed the poor nor his body to be burned, and yet even these, without love, are nothing. But you want to receive everything from God in the Sacrament, and you do not wish to pour out again in love. No one will give a hand to another and everyone is thinking about himself. Nobody bothers about the poor.

You have heard enough on this for a long time back. All my books are full of urging faith and love. If you do not love one another, God will let loose a great plague upon you. He will not have his word preached in vain. You tempt God too much, my friends. If these words had been preached to our fathers, they might have responded differently, and if now one went to preach in this fashion to many in the cloisters, they would accept it more joyously, but you do not take this to heart. Instead, you go gawking after some trumpery. I commend you to God.

Fellowship

[1519]

THE MEANING OF THIS SACRAMENT is the communion of all saints. The participation in bread and wine is the sign of fellowship with Christ and all the saints just as a man on becoming a citizen is given a certificate testifying that he belongs to a town and a community. When you share in this Sacrament you must take to yourself all that may befall the community. Give your heart over to love and learn that this is a sacrament of love. In all its forms it suggests and kindles fellowship. Just as grains of wheat are kneaded together and assume one form in the bread, just as grapes and berries when pressed give up their individual shapes and become a common body, so should Christians be a single spiritual body.

[1528]

I HAVE THE SAME FAITH, teaching, and Sacrament with you. Likewise I have the same weakness, ignorance, transgressions, and poverty with you. Are you naked? Then I am also, and I can have no peace until I have clothed you. Are you hungry and thirsty? Thus we come into one kitchen and my food is yours and your hunger and thirst are mine. Again, are you a sinner? Then so am I. Or am I joyous and strong? Then I take on your sadness and weakness and rest not until you are like me. Thus, your joy is my joy and likewise, your sadness is mine.

[1519]

CHRIST WITH ALL HIS SAINTS assumes in love our form and fights with us against sin, death, and all evil. Thereby, we are kindled and assume his form, abandoning ourselves to his righteousness, being kneaded into the fellowship of his benefits and of our miseries as one loaf, one body, and one drink. How great a Sacrament this is, as Paul says, that Christ should be one flesh and one bone with his church. (Ephesians 5:32). So ought we also in the same love to transform ourselves and take to ourselves the needs and the transgressions of other Christians, and whatever we have of good, we should leave to them that they may also enjoy it. Then we shall be made over into each other and fashioned into a fellowship of love without which this change cannot take place.

Arrest and Trial

On What to Meditate

TODAY IS PASSION SUNDAY. It is good once a year to read through the whole story of the Passion. If I go for two days without thinking of Christ, I become faint and sluggish. What, then, would become of those who for a year at a time do not hear of him?

Yet, even those who hear the Word are not awakened. The Passion of Christ has been read, sung, and preached, but to what end? One may say that it is both proclaimed and hidden. Few of those who gladly hear reflect upon the meaning. They go to church, listen to the recital of the Passion, and as they came in, so they go out. They are delighted to hear that Christ our Lord shed his blood for us, but should we tell them not to covet, to grasp, to fornicate—then the whole Rhine would be ablaze. They retort: "You should not scold us. We are all Christians. God has saved us from our sins." Thus, a particle of candid truth stirs up resentment. Such is the nature of this preaching—that though it is publicly proclaimed, scarcely does it ever lodge in the heart.

The Gospels are discrepant with regard to the external events in the garden of Gethsemane. The frivolous fasten on details of this sort and lose the essentials. If, for example, we concentrate on the crown of thorns, the nails, and the pieces of the cross, we miss the true use of the Passion. I wish the cross had never been discovered, and perhaps it is not genuine, for the devil is fond of drawing us from Christ to a piece of wood. I really believe that the story of the finding of the true cross is all made up. I wish, also, that the bones of Christ and of all saints were under the earth in some unknown place like those of Moses. Let us then center on Christ and not bother about the Jews, the house, the supper, Judas, and the arrest. You do not need to go to Jerusalem and look at the footprints of Jesus. What good is it to have seen the house of Pilate or the steps on which Christ fainted? The question is how Christ looks upon you.

> *"The chief priests and the scribes sought how they might take him by craft, and put him to death. But they said, Not on the feast day, lest there be an uproar of the people."*
> (MARK 14:1-2)

They were afraid to do it at the time of the feast when so many Jews came up to Jerusalem. They would make thirty times one hundred thousand, without women and children. I doubt whether there are so many people in all Germany. So, the chief priests said: "See how the people hang upon him. We shall have to be crafty and strike at the right time if the plot is to succeed."

Anointing in Bethany
(MARK 14:3-9)

ON THE EVE prior to Passion Week, Jesus was in Bethany. We read that Mary took ointment. It was an old custom to wash with

perfumed water not only the face but also the hands and the feet. Mary had purchased a very costly vessel. In our day we have wild nard, but not the kind mixed with balsam of that time, which was very precious. It was not an ointment but a sweet-smelling perfume with herbs. She poured it over his head and raiment. It spoiled nothing but made everything pure and of a sweet smell. The Lord suffered it. He took no pleasure in the perfume, for his heart was full of heaviness and thoughts of death. In six days, he would die. He who knows certainly that he will die a shameful death on a particular day will take no delight in gold, pearl necklaces, and clothes, for his spirit is in deep anguish because he must shed his blood. Piping, singing, and dancing do not help here. But Christ permitted what she did. Mary believed him to be a prophet and meant it well. He was wrestling with death and took no delight in this of itself.

The Judas Iscariot, the son of Simon, thought to himself: "Mary wastes money. She pours out the perfume even on his feet and this rose water costs so much. Why did she not use lye or soap? This perfume might have been sold for three hundred groschen and given to the poor." A groschen, by the way, corresponded to a Nuremberg pound and came to about thirty-five gulden. Judas probably said to himself: "That is too much. With this amount of money I could have fed twenty-four people and could indeed have cared for sixty persons for a month, and now it is gone all in one hour." This all sounds very plausible, and it is just the way the pope raises money to go against the Turks. Now, of course, fighting the Turks and giving alms to the poor are good, but the pope means it like Judas.

Christ said: "Let her alone. . . . She is come aforehand to anoint my body to the burying." He pointed to his death, though she did not understand it. These thirty-five gulden, he would say, are a farewell. If it were for the last time, I would give all at once everything that I might have given in thirty years as a token of love to Christ's Word.

Washing of the Disciples' Feet

(JOHN 13:1-20)

CHRIST SENT THE DISCIPLES into the city to prepare the Passover supper for him. And when they were gathered, he took "a basin, and began to wash the disciples' feet." In this, one sees what a person he was; how inconceivably friendly. "Ye call me Master and Lord," he said, "and ye say well; for so I am. If I then, your Lord and Master, have washed your feet; ye also ought to wash one another's feet."

There was no need that Christ should have done this. He could have said to Peter, "You go and wash Judas's feet; I am the Master." But instead he subjected himself and emptied himself of his majesty and behaved as a servant. Then Peter undertook to instruct him and said, "You are the Master, and I am the servant," but Christ rebuffed him and went on to explain the meaning of the foot washing.

What a contrast between Christ washing the disciples' feet and the pope having his toe kissed! Christ well foresaw that the successors of the apostles would wish to receive service, but he intended that all Christians and, especially the successors of the apostles, should render service. This does not refer specifically to foot washing, though I like it and would gladly have it continued,

but when it comes to theatrical foot washing, that is sheer ostentation. If you really want to wash the feet of the poor, take them into your house, feed them, and clothe them, and do it the whole year through.

In washing the feet of the disciples, Christ gave an example of love, for this is the nature of love—to serve and to be subject to another. If one esteems another more highly than himself, then love and all good works are there. Jesus said, "Ye also ought to wash one another's feet." Thus Christ made himself the lowliest. One sees here genuine love, for the heart is with the loved one and desires to do his pleasure. In this, one finds sympathy, mercy, brotherliness, and a helping hand, but then the devil breaks in and says through the pope that these are not enough; that they are just ordinary commands; that one should go farther, become a monk, put on a cowl, and fast for six days. Even faith is called an ordinary thing, and we are told to do something extraordinary. Faith is merely for the heathen, but Christians must be urged to do something more, to take a cowl and the like. As for myself, I have scarcely made a beginning in faith. To the very grave, I shall have to go on learning. I am not concerned about works. I pray simply, "Help me that I may firmly believe." If that happens, then bring on all the cowls and everything else the pope has commanded. So, then, love your neighbor and esteem him higher than yourself. But then again they come and say that this is only an ordinary command. I reply: "Where are those who have kept it? Have you? You have not."

It is a mighty love that puts us all to confusion that the divine majesty should so humble himself. Fie, how shameful if we do not take it to heart! But who knows whether his heart is pure. Look at Judas. There he sits like a lord full of the devil. And the Lord God goes down on his knees as a servant in front of him. If the kaiser should kiss a beggar's feet, that would be a stinking humility and not worthy to be named in comparison with what was done by the divine majesty. These examples are too deep for us to think of imitating.

Gethsemane

AFTER THE SUPPER, we read in John's Gospel (John 18:1) that "he went forth with his disciples over the brook of Cedron, where was a garden." This was the Garden of Gethsemane. Why did Jesus not flee? He did not evade the cross. He could have done so sevenfold, but he continued his way according to his custom. From this we see that one should neither seek nor shun the cross. No one has been given his body in order to crucify it. In that case, God would not have made the body healthy. The purpose of the body is to labor as a servant in order to provide food, clothes, work, and rest. The body is to be kept in subjection, but we are not to court affliction.

"And Judas also, who betrayed him, knew the place." Judas, then, having received a band of men and officers from the chief priests, came thither. Judas had two bands, one from the priests, the other from the Romans, that none might call him a rebel. Christ was then abandoned by the angels and by the authorities, and even his disciples fled. How everything was reversed! When he preached in Jerusalem, no one dared to touch him. Now the

people and the magistrates forsook him. That is the way it is bound to be. If our Saxon princes were overcome and Wittenberg were besieged, we should then find out who were good Christians. Those who now are Evangelical would certainly desert and go over to the enemy, as the people then did to the Pharisees. He who would be a Christian must seek help that he may be strong in himself.

"Then Simon Peter having a sword drew it."
(John 18:10-11)

All too readily men grasp a sword. They forget how great a difference there is between the one to whom a thing is commanded and him to whom it is not. God does not slumber. He knows how government is to be conducted. When an injustice occurs the mob is disposed to step in because the old Adam is a great fool. That is what Müntzer did. Peter had the best intentions. He was moved by love and loyalty to his Master. He said, "My Lord is in danger; I am his sworn disciple." The world could not blame him for that, but Christ did, as if to say: "There is a government in Jerusalem. They will deal with this fellow. The sword has not been given to you."

Now as a matter of fact, the government did wrong, and Peter did right. Whom should I then commend, the one who had the authority and did wrong? Obviously not, but also not the one who having no authority did right. Even if you could raise the dead, the sword would not on that account be committed to you. Here is the word, "Put up thy sword into the sheath." Of course, it is true that Peter was defending an innocent man and that he had the best of intentions, but you must leave questions of right

to the jurists and inquire what has been committed to you. Christ would rather suffer wrong than overturn God's order, and God would rather have an unjust magistracy than an unjust people. The reason is that the mob gets out of hand and heads fly in all directions. That is why Peter, despite his good intentions, was wrong, and Pilate, the Pharisees, and the godless were right. The peasants had the very best case when they said, "Who can stand for this?" But they ought also to have said, "We have not received the command." You have no business to say: "My heart is right. My intentions are good; the case is just." But rather you should say, "Have I been commissioned?" Unfortunately in the world everything is upside down. Those who have the good intentions have not the authority, and those who have the authority have not the good intentions.

Trial Before Annas and Peter's Denial

JESUS WAS TAKEN first to the house of Annas. Now Annas had a daughter given to Caiaphas to wife. She was the first woman in Jerusalem, and Caiaphas was a bigwig and, at that time, the high priest. As for rank, I would rather have been Caiaphas than the pope at Rome. But now let us come to theology. If Caiaphas could not be believed, then let the devil believe the papists, the councils, and the bishops. The moral is that you cannot believe anyone because of his high station. The jurists have boasted of their pope, that such loftiness cannot err, but take Caiaphas. He had a higher place than the pope and the emperor, but not only was he wrong and Annas with him, but they were the worst idiots on earth, for they crucified the Son of God.

"And Simon Peter followed Jesus."
(JOHN 18:15)

I believe that in the whole story of the Passion no part is so carefully portrayed as Peter's denial, and there is good reason, for no article is so hard to believe as the forgiveness of sins. That is because the other articles do not affect us, as for example, "I believe in God the Father Almighty" and so on, but the forgiveness of sins touches me and touches you. There are other articles that are hard to understand, as that the bread is his body or that the Holy Spirit appeared at the baptism, but this one is the hardest. Because it is so hard and a man is so terrified by hell and judgment, therefore the forgiveness of sins had to be drastically portrayed in Peter, that every man might take comfort.

"One of the officers struck Jesus with the palm of his hand
. . . and Jesus answered, Why smitest thou me?"
(JOHN 18:22-23)

This text has been utilized to turn God's command into a counsel of perfection. In the Sermon on the Mount, Jesus said, "If anyone strike thee on the one cheek, turn to him the other also, etc." This is the command of the gospel, that one should not resist evil nor avenge oneself. But now the cloisters and the universities have interpreted this as if it were not a command but only good advice. He who is so inclined, say they, may keep it, for it is merely counsel and not a binding word. By way of corroboration they adduce this text and say: "Did Christ turn the other cheek? Did he not rather reprove the servant? Therefore, the injunction to turn the other cheek is no command, for in that case, Jesus would have done it."

The apparent discrepancy is to be understood in terms of the two kingdoms, the civil and the spiritual. In the one the emperor rules over rascals. In the other the Son of God over Christians. Christ will accept only those whose hearts are right, for he has only the word and no rod or sword, but the civil government has to do with rascals. When they do wrong, they have to be constrained by blows. Otherwise no one could be safe in his own house. When one commits a crime the executioner must take off his head. Christ, then, means to say, "My teaching does not apply to the emperor, but only to the children of God." It was to these that he gave his teaching about turning the other cheek, giving away the cloak, and going the second mile, that is to say, overcoming evil with good. The word of Christ is advice when addressed to the world and the emperor, but when spoken to the Christian in the realm of the spirit, it is a command.

You reply, "But Christ did not follow this command; instead he said, 'Why do you strike me?'" But examine now this text more carefully and observe that Christ offered not merely the other cheek but his whole body to be scourged and crucified. Turning the other cheek and reproving in words are quite distinct. A Christian must suffer, but the word is placed in his mouth that he should declare what is unjust. If a robber assailed me in the woods and said, "Your cloak is mine," I should not agree with him, for in that case I should share his crime. The hand and the mouth need to be distinguished. The hand may give, but the mouth cannot approve.

Similarly when the world condemns our teaching and would take our lives, what, then, are we to do? Like Christ we should suffer not merely the blow on the cheek but burning itself, but if we say to the judge, "You are right in burning us," that would be to betray Christ and deny everything for which he died. As for my person, I will suffer, but as for my teaching I am unafraid. This Scripture is an example that we should be bold. The hangman may be my master, but my teaching is right. That is what Jesus said to the servant, and that is what we should say to the tyrants. This gripes the devil and wrings him as if he had been robbed of half of hell.

Trial before Pilate

(JOHN 18:28 TO 19:16)

And Pilate said, "What accusation bring ye against this man?"

THE ACCUSERS WERE CONVICTED not only by their own consciences, but by this very heathen. I would not exchange comfort for ten Turkish empires. When Pilate asked, "What accusation bring ye against this man?" their consciences writhed. That is what happens in our case. Our opponents resist the truth and cry out against us, but if there were a proper hearing, our innocence would come to light. The mob did not present an accusation, namely, that Jesus claimed to be their king. That was the only charge which Pilate took seriously. The worst scoundrels could not have devised a more damaging accusation, just as today the gospel is said to be insurrectionary. The rascals knew the charge was not true that Christ desired to be a king. This is our comfort, that our Lord had to endure the charge of insurrection because of his word.

Pilate called Jesus and said, "Art thou the King of the Jews?" Jesus answered him, "Sayest thou this of thyself, or did others tell thee of me?" This sounds proud, but it was not. Jesus was denying the accusation. It was as if he said: "You know yourself, Pilate, whether I am a king, that is, whether I am a rebel. I call your own conscience to witness. You did not say this of yourself, for your own eyes give the answer. You see that I am bound. I have no crowd about me ready to unsheath weapons. I have the air of a prisoner." Pilate was somewhat irritated at this answer, though it was necessary and not proud, and this was the way in which I

must talk to the emperor, "Does your Majesty say this of yourself, or did someone else tell it to you?"

Pilate answered: "Am I a Jew? Thine own nation and the chief priests have delivered thee unto me: What hast thou done?" Then the Lord gave the finest and clearest answer: "My Kingdom does no harm to you nor to the emperor. I am no rebel. That you can see with your own eyes and no one can say anything to the contrary."

Then Jesus made his confession, "My Kingdom is not of this world." That was a very dangerous confession, for at the very same time he both denied and confessed that he was a king. He admitted that he came to make a revolution and yet was not a revolutionary, for the gospel does not come without revolution. "Think you that I am come to bring peace on earth?" He said, "I say, no, but division."

In just the same fashion we are revolutionists now. We preach that everyone should obey his lord and in this we are peaceful and peaceable. We teach and pray for peace. We help the emperor in his kingdom and then we upset his kingdom when we say that the Kingdom of Christ is higher than the kingdom of the Emperor Charles. Life and goods we submit in obedience, but we preach the gospel and this divides hearts from hearts. In this comes the revolution, that the father has a different faith from the son, not that they live in different houses, for Christ did not say, "I will send a fire and burn their houses down," but rather that in the same house there should be division. The point is not that children should not obey their parents but that they will believe differently. The gospel is a kingdom, and it effects a revolution, only it is a spiritual revolution.

Pilate said: "Ye have a custom, that I should release unto you one at the passover: will ye therefore that I release unto you the King of the Jews? Then cried they all again, saying, Not this man, but Barabbas." So is it today. Barabbas is made a town counselor, a bishop, a dean, and a provost. You cannot expect the world to be any different from what it was in Christ's day. We are serving in an inn where the devil is the keeper, the world is his wife, the lusts of the world are the household, and all of them put together are against the gospel. It is a shame that the world prefers murder, adultery, faithlessness, trickery, guile, lying, and deception to the truth. They would rather bathe the world in blood than have the truth.

"Then Pilate therefore took Jesus, and scourged him. And the soldiers platted a crown of thorns, and put it on his head, and they put on him a purple robe."

These soldiers did more than was commanded them. Scourging was the practice, but in addition, to please the priests, they gave him a crown of thorns, dressed him in a purple robe, and hailed him as King of the Jews because of his confession that he was a king. So they had a vaudeville giving him a crown and the imperial purple. What more cruel, biting, venomous, devilish mockery could they have devised! And that is what happens to the gospel now and ever will. Scourging hurts, but taunts cut deeper.

"Pilate therefore went forth again, and saith unto them, Behold, I bring him forth to you, that ye may know that I find no fault in him."

This is an invincible witness of the truth for Jesus, that Pilate confessed once, twice, thrice, yes, even six times that he found no fault in him. Likewise, we today should have such a teaching that our opponents will have to say, "It is indeed right, though we will have none of it."

"The Jews answered him, We have a law, and by our law he ought to die, because he made himself the Son of God."

Then Pilate trembled more. It was not that he believed him to be the Son of God, but he thought: "The Romans do have many gods. Who knows?" We find that the heathen often claimed gods to have appeared in human form. So now Pilate thought, "Suppose he is a god?" He said then to Jesus: "Who are thou? Whence art thou?" But Jesus gave him no answer.

"Then saith Pilate unto him, Speakest thou not unto me? knowest thou not that I have power?"

Pilate trusted to and boasted in his might like a heathen. Similarly today there are those who want power to make and to break in the church according to their will. Christ now could no longer be silent. Where speech seemed timely, he spoke not, but where silence appeared seemly, he spoke. When Pilate claimed power, then Jesus told him he had no power. "Thou couldst have no power at all against me, were it not given thee from above."

By this, Christ showed that one should not be silent in declaring the truth before the big lords. Christ did not, however, say, "Pilate, you have no power over me." Rather he said: "You have power, as you yourself say, but there is another point. You do not have it from yourself but it is given to you." In this, Christ reproved Pilate because he was so overweening and this we, too, must do to our Pilates. We are accused of despising the majesty of the emperor and the princes, but when they tell us we ought to say, "Gracious lord, what you do is right," that we will not do. There is a great difference between suffering injustice and in keeping still. Suffer, yes—be silent, no—for I must witness to the truth, and if we must die for the truth, still we must confess and reprove the lie with the mouth. If we say, "Dear lords, you are not behaving like Christian princes and spiritual fathers but rather like murderous apostates from Christ and enemies of the gospel"— if we say this, we are accused of treason, but I must speak. This is the truth. He who speaks against it is against God. He who goes against it is an enemy of the gospel.

Now if Pilate had had a grain of courage, he would have freed Jesus. Nature and reason teach that one should not do wrong for someone else. It will not do to say: "I stole your cow but not for myself. I did it for your enemy." So here Pilate manifestly did wrong for the sake of the mob. Yet, he did try to set Jesus free, but the mob said, "Let this man go, and thou art not Caesar's friend." The mob had first claimed that Jesus was disloyal because he wanted to be a king. Pilate saw through this. Then they charged that Christ made himself out to be the Son of God. That, too, was unimpressive. Now they reverted to the first charge and heightened it by saying that if he wants to be a king, he is against the emperor, and if you set him free, we will write to Rome and accuse you of favoring a rebel.

Then Pilate wilted. "Thou are not Caesar's friend." That is the word that causes men to fall away like autumn leaves. Flesh and blood cannot bear to be the emperor's enemy. This made Pilate blind. So today there are many good Evangelicals, but they do not care enough for the gospel to risk limb and life. They follow Pilate. He has many children. Pilate then asked no more questions but passed judgment, saying to the crowd, "Behold your king!" He was saying as it were: "Fie, shame on you all! If you were the right sort, you would come armed to drive me and all my men out of your city because I crucified your king. You ought to defend him against me, but you drag him in, that I may execute him when I would rather set him free." Matthew records that Pilate washed his hands and said, "I am innocent of his blood." Yet, he turned him over to their will. He shared their guilt, even though he confessed Christ's innocence. The justice of the world can do no better.

Christ then was condemned not on account of his teaching but as a rebel against the imperial majesty, and he who would follow the gospel must endure the charge of revolution.

The Crucifixion

Then, "bearing his cross, he went forth."
(JOHN 19:17)

SO JOHN RECORDS. The other Gospels say the Master could go
no farther, and Simon of Cyrene was compelled to carry the cross
for him. The painters who show Simon helping him are mistak-
en. Christ carried the cross himself to the gate, and from then on
Simon took over. We are not so cruel as were the Orientals,
for we do not make criminals carry their wheels, but it is written
to show the great cost of the redemption of our sins. Christ was
not simply condemned but had even to carry the very cross on
which he should die.

He went forth to a spot called Golgotha, the place of the
skull—in Latin, *Calvary.* At Wittenberg, we call it the gallows.
It was the common place of execution. Not only had he to carry
his cross but also be executed with two criminals—highway ban-
dits, murderers who are today executed with the sword and wheel
as breakers of the peace. Christ must be crucified not only with
them but between them. Pilate did not command this, but the

soldiers did it to please the high priest. There hung the Lord, a robber, a thief, a rebel, a murderer. All this the unspotted Lamb must bear, and all this was for us. Our sins lay upon his head and through him many robbers have been blessed, as was one of the two on that day.

Above his cross was inscribed: "JESUS OF NAZARETH THE KING OF THE JEWS." To announce the nature of the crime was a good custom. The heathen took their justice seriously. No one could be condemned without being accused, and no one was executed without having been heard. And this, too, was excellent that at an execution a placard was placed upon the gallows or cross that all might know the offense. Christ was charged with being the King of the Jews. Today we still write it above the cross, though now it has become a title of honor, just as his cross and death have come to be esteemed.

"Now there stood by the cross of Jesus his mother."
(JOHN 19:25)

What agony Mary endured as she watched his suffering none can comprehend. In all history there is no other account of a woman who followed her son when he must suffer so frightfully. She saw him crowned with thorns, spat upon, and hanged. Truly the sword of Simeon must have gone through her heart. A mother can scarcely stand it if her child falls from a bench or bleeds from the ear. Where shall we find a mother who could see such things as Mary? She could not speak but must watch all the tortures and hear all the revilings as they gave him vinegar to drink and diced for his clothing. To be sure, the Holy Spirit gave her comfort, but other mothers would have fainted. And for Christ, to see his mother suffer was one of the greatest parts of his pain, that nothing should be lacking in his suffering.

In the case of the thief we have an example of Christ's forgiveness. The thief reproved his fellow, saying, "Do you not fear God, you who are in the same condemnation?" These were simple words, but the heart of the thief was greater than heaven and earth. He did not look upon the weakness of Christ. Instead, he saw what cannot be seen, that Christ was a king. Be not ashamed to become a Christian after the manner of this thief, for he was the first saint in the New Testament through the Passion of Christ. For him, Christ prayed upon the cross. We might all be Christians like him. God grant that we may!

Yet this example is not so easy as it seems. He who would come to Christ must feel himself to be a sinner and believe it. Here is the point at which the faith of the thief had an art above any art of which I am capable. When sin and punishment come together, to say that it is right is the art that no cleric possesses. The thief accepted the punishment and bore it willingly, as if he would say: "I deserve it. I will bear it gladly." He who can do that has already conquered, and he who cannot do it is in great danger. The thief did nothing more than to believe and pray. There was no fasting, no pilgrimage. He turned his eyes to the Lord and said, "Lord, remember me when thou comest into thy Kingdom." These are words of faith. He confessed that Christ was King and that he had a Kingdom and asked to be remembered and that was all.

"And Christ prayed, Father, forgive them; for they know
not what they do."
(Luke 23:24)

Who can express such love? His heart was so full of the fire of love that no one can comprehend. In pain and shame he acted as though he felt them not and was thinking only of our sin and God's wrath. Is that not love? He burned and writhed beneath the weight, the spear, the blood, the shame, and wounds, and yet he said, "Father, forgive them; for they know not what they do." Here there is a loveliness that only the eyes of the spirit can discern. He was esteemed a robber, a rascal, a reprobate above all reprobates, yet in the heart he was fairer than the sun.

"There was darkness over all the land."

(MATTHEW 27:45)

The darkness lasted for three hours, from eleven until two o'clock. He cried, *"Eli, Eli, lama sabachthani?"* It was not merely the suffering but the reproach that hurt. They taunted him: "He trusted in God; let God save him." These were barbed words which smote not only his ears but his heart. He felt what his cry expressed, that he was forsaken by God, as if to say: "God is just. He would not abandon a just man. You must then be his enemy." Reason always comes to this conclusion on the basis of appearance. His enemies argued, "God lets him hang upon the cross, therefore, he must be an accursed heretic." Such words wrung his heart, for we must remember that Christ was a true man. To me also the words would be very bitter if the devil said, "You are mine." I would collapse. The anguish that Christ experienced here drove him to cry out, "My God, my God, why hast thou forsaken me." Just as a man, when a sword is about to be driven through his neck, lets out in terror a cry of death, so also Christ. In this he was a man as other men. The Passion that Christ suffered from words was even worse than from blows. It is also with us when the godless reproach us with venomous gibes and threaten us with the wrath of God. They talk as if it were so, and that stings.

The three hours of darkness were frightful. To Christ it seemed that on his account God had blotted out the sun. That is why Christ cried out. His accusers should have been shaken by his death cry, but they were only more hardened and said: "The living God is his enemy. That is why he turns to the dead Elijah." Such reproaches hurt Christ more than all the pain. He felt it all as a man.

> *"And one ran and took a sponge and filled it with vinegar,*
> *and put it on a reed, and gave him to drink."*
> (MATTHEW 27:48)

What mockery! They should have comforted him. The devil emptied all his wrath upon this man. Read all the recitals of dying, and you will not find anything more terrible that this, that one who was forsaken but God and all creatures should be comforted with vinegar.

> *"And Jesus cried with a loud voice and yielded up the ghost."*
> (MATTHEW 27:50)

Even if it were an animal, the onlooker would be deeply moved, but when it is an innocent man and when he is the Son of God! If one should properly consider this, one's heart would burst that God's Son, creator of all things, should let out a cry of death. This is above all sense and understanding. We cannot get to the bottom of it our life long.

We should not center our attention, however, upon what Christ suffered but rather upon why he suffered, and the answer is, "for my sake." I am the one who by my sins have deserved that God be my enemy and mock me, even when I cry that the sun should no more shine, the earth no more bear me, and the rocks be rent. When sins are made plain and the conscience is touched, then a man finds out all that Christ suffered here. Then he, too, will say, "Why hast thou forsaken me?" Therefore, everything that Christ suffered is to be referred to our souls, and the more we exalt the Passion the more clearly do we see our own condemnation. Yet, "I will not be afraid for the terror by night, and though the sun should not shine and I be in the shadow of death, I will fear no evil, for thou art with me. Though the earth cry out against me, I will not fear, for I know that Christ has conquered."

> *"And the veil of the temple was rent in twain from the top to the bottom; and the earth did quake, and the rocks rent; and the graves were opened."*
> (MATTHEW 27:51)

The veil of the temple was rent, the darkness on which no one might look became light. While the veil remained, the gospel was hidden and not openly preached, but now with the death of Christ, all that was of the old Adam and the law was dead and done away. Now that I no longer see an angry judge, but that God has given his Son for me, I behold upon the cross the fiery, fatherly love of God.

"The earth quaked."

(MATTHEW 27:51)

When the veil was rent and God was made known as Father, then the whole earth shook as we see it today, for now the gospel is preached and the earth quakes and the world persecutes us. The rocks are rent. That means the hearts formerly under the law. The Scripture speaks of stony hearts. Through the power of the gospel, when grace is preached, hearts are rent by love.

"And the graves were opened."

(MATTHEW 27:52)

His death swallowed up death and the very centurion said, "Truly this was the Son of God." He is an amazing king. Other kings are strong in life, he in death. While he lived he was trodden upon, and his enemies took his life. When he was dead the centurion trembled and commenced to be a Christian. The blood of Christ brings to life not only dead bodies but also the souls of prisoners. The disciples had fled, but this centurion began to confess Christ without fear of all the high priests or of what Pilate and the council might say. Who, then, was master here? Was it not the death of Christ that gave the heathen centurion a new spirit? This is the power of the Passion that it makes men bold to confess Christ. We should see from this that through his death he is the Lord of life and death. Whether, then, we live or die, we are in God's hand.

"When even was come, there came a rich man of Arimathea, named Joseph."

(MATTHEW 27:57)

He had heard that Christ was more powerful in death than in life, and that this heathen had confessed him. This Joseph was a disciple of Jesus but before had been very timid. He was a member of Sanhedrin. Mark implies that he had absented himself when judgment was taken against Jesus because he lacked the courage to attend and say that the deed was wrong, but now that Christ was dead, he came and asked for the body. That was a brave act in the teeth of the leaders of church and state. Suppose somebody today should go against the emperor like that? Joseph could do no greater honor to Jesus than to bury him in his own grave. Such high courage sprang from the death of Christ.

Let us now meditate a moment on the Passion of Christ. Some do so falsely in that they merely rail against Judas and the Jews. Some carry crucifixes to protect themselves from water, fire, and sword, and turn the suffering of Christ into an amulet against suffering. Some weep and that is the end of it. The true contemplation is that in which the heart is crushed and the conscience smitten. You must be overwhelmed by the frightful wrath of God who so hated sin that he spared not his only-begotten Son. What can the sinner expect if the beloved Son was so afflicted? It must be an inexpressible and unendurable yearning that causes God's Son himself so to suffer. Ponder this and you will tremble, and the more you ponder, the deeper you will tremble.

Take this to heart and doubt not that you are the one who killed Christ. Your sins certainly did, and when you see the nails driven through his hands, be sure that you are pounding, and when the thorns pierce his brow, know that they are your evil thoughts. Consider that if one thorn pierced Christ you deserve one hundred thousand.

The whole value of the meditation of the suffering of Christ lies in this, that man should come to the knowledge of himself and sink and tremble. If you are so hardened that you do not tremble, then you have reason to tremble. Pray to God that he may soften your heart and make fruitful your meditation upon the suffering of Christ, for we of ourselves are incapable of proper reflection unless God instill it.

But if one does meditate rightly on the suffering of Christ for a day, an hour, or even a quarter of an hour, this we may confidently say is better than a whole year of fasting, days of psalm singing, yes, than even one hundred Masses, because this reflection changes the whole man and makes him new, as once he was in baptism.

If, then, Christ is so firmly planted in your heart, and if you are become an enemy to sin out of love and not fear, then henceforth, the suffering of Christ, which began as a sacrament, may continue lifelong as an example. When tribulation and sickness assail you, think how slight these are compared to the thorns and the nails of Christ. If you are thwarted, remember how he was bound and dragged. If pride besets you, see how the Lord was mocked and with robbers despised. If unchastity incites your flesh, recall how his flesh was scourged, pierced, and smitten. If hate, envy, and vengeance tempt you, think how Christ for you and all his enemies interceded with tears, though he might rather have avenged himself. If you are afflicted and cannot have your way, take heart and say, "Why should I not suffer when my Lord sweat blood for very anguish."

Astounding it is that the cross of Christ has so fallen into forgetfulness, for is it not forgetfulness of cross when no one wishes to suffer but rather to enjoy himself and evade the cross? You must personally experience suffering with Christ. He suffered for your sake and should you not suffer for his sake, as well as for your own?

Two texts in the Old Testament apply to Christ. The first is, "Thou art fairer than the children of men" (Psalm 45:2), and the second is, "He hath no form nor comeliness" (Isaiah 53:2). Evidently these passages must be understood in differing senses. To the eyes of the flesh, he was the lowest among the sons of men, a derision, and to the eyes of the spirit there was none fairer than he. The eyes of the flesh cannot see this. What, then, is the nature of this beauty? It is wisdom and love, light for the understanding, and power for the soul, for in suffering and dying Christ displayed all the wisdom and the truth with which the understanding can be adorned. All the treasures of wisdom and knowledge are hidden in him, and they are hidden because they are visible only to the eye of the spirit.

The greater and the more wonderful is the excellence of his love by contrast with the lowliness of his form, the hate and pain of Passion. Herein we come to know both God and ourselves. His beauty is his own and through it we learn to know him. His uncomeliness and Passion are ours, and in them we know ourselves, for what he suffered in the flesh, we must inwardly suffer in the spirit. He has in truth borne our stripes. Here, then, in an unspeakably clear mirror you see yourself. You must know that through your sins you are as uncomely and mangled as you see him here.

If we consider the persons, we ought to suffer a thousand and again a thousand times more than Christ because he is God and we are dust and ashes, yet it is the reverse. He, who had a thousand and again a thousand times less need, has taken upon himself a thousand and again a thousand times more than we. No understanding can fathom nor tongue can express, no writing can record, but only the inward feeling can grasp, what is involved in the suffering of Christ.

The Resurrection

The Empty Tomb

"Who shall roll away the stone?"

(MARK 16:3)

THE ANGEL WHO SAT on the stone and who had driven away the guards was gone. The women thought, "Who will roll away the stone?" They were distressed and supposed they had come for nothing. Still, great love had brought them to the tomb, and they saw that the guards were gone and the stone rolled away. But this did not seem to them to augur any good, for they thought that Jesus' enemies had taken away the body to prevent the disciples from doing so. The women entered with heavy hearts, and while they stood, two men appeared before them in shining raiment at whom they dared not look for terror. The angel said, "Why seek ye the living among the dead?"

"He is not here."

(MARK 16:6)

A Christian should be where Christ is. If Christ is not here, a Christian should not be here. That is why no one can find Christ or a Christian in any particular set of rules. He is not here. He has left behind the graveclothes, namely, worldly justice, wisdom, piety, law, and the like. You are not to seek him in these things which are to be found on earth. You won't find him in any Carthusian or in any other monastic cowl. You will not find him in fasting, watchings, vestments. These are all graveclothes. Also, all customs and usages of the fathers and the jurists, the wise and the godly, and whatever else there may be, these are only graveclothes. He is not here. He never puts on graveclothes, nor can a Christian.

But now some jump to the wrong conclusion from this, and the Radicals say, since this is so, that we are above all things and not bound to this or that, then, let us do what we please. That is what the peasants did in their insurrection. They wrecked castles, cloisters, and sacked cellars, and all this they called Christian freedom, but you never make yourselves Christians by

demolishing cloisters and despising the government. A Christian is, indeed, above everything on earth, regardless of his station, whether lord or serf, prince or servant, matron or maid. He is a Christian because he clings to the One who died and rose again and is no longer here.

But a Christian has still to live with other people. My body still must have wife, children, house, clothes, and food. God does not intend by the gospel to overturn the civil order. He wants the spirit and the heart to rule, but he has left the hands and the feet as he made them. If I believe on Christ, I am at home in my fatherland, but in the body I am a guest. Then, I must behave like other people, uphold the good of the world, and help to maintain the common peace, and, in addition to that, although I am free, I must nevertheless be a servant to every man. I have hands and feet and tongue, eyes, ears; they all belong together, and with them I must be a servant and so live that I may be helpful to others.

The Radicals should preach this and not mix everything up. They are looking for outward freedom, but Christian freedom does not belong on earth, but rather to a better land. Whether, then, you are husband, wife, son, daughter, lord, or servant, do what falls to you. Believe me, it is very difficult to keep apart these two kingdoms.

The women then returned fearful to the city. They had seen indeed the angel but did not listen to him, for one that is in danger of death can scarcely take hold of the words of life.

The dear apostles heard indeed the words of the women that the grave was open and that an angel had been seen. The first they believed readily enough, but that Christ really was alive appeared to them to be an idle tale. The apostles would say, "We think you are a silly crew." The apostles could not see the living Christ because the dead and buried Christ was so impressed upon their thoughts. In periods of depression, it is always so, and if anyone says the contrary, one takes it for a fairy tale.

Mary told Peter and the disciples, "They have taken away the Lord, and we know not where they have laid him" (John 20:2). Though all the women said this, the disciples did not yet believe, and the women then allowed themselves to be persuaded that it was only a fantasy and that they had been deceived. The words of the angel were thus in vain, but Mary Magdalene kept on saying, "They have taken away my Lord."

Then went Peter and John to the tomb. John, who records this very properly, gives Peter the honor of the first place. The papists infer from this that Peter was above John. Now when these came to the grave, they found their unbelief confirmed that the body of the Lord had been taken away as Magdalene had said. Peter then certainly thought: "Christ surely would not have arranged the graveclothes in this fashion. Someone else must have done it." At the sight of the napkin he was doubly sure. So they went forth in unbelief. Why? Because they did not credit the Scripture and did not realize that it predicts the resurrection. The disciples then returned to the city. This was the second visit to the tomb.

In the Garden

THE WOMEN CONFERRED with Peter and John, but their doubt was only as to who had taken away the body, whether members of the council or Pilate. There was no thought of the resurrection, not so much as a hairbreadth. While the other women had departed, Mary Magdalene remained in the garden. She stayed in the tomb, went in and out, peered, saw two angels, and finally the Lord himself, whom she did not know. This is something to ponder, that the Lord first appeared to Mary Magdalene, and it is something to consider that he first appeared to a woman. It is a great comfort that women are the type of those who hear the gospel. In these women there is a great unconquerable strength out of the Word that stands firm against all the assaults of Satan. Those who accept the gospel are the Magdalenes, that is, the weak. The Word that they hear cuts through death and sin.

Mary spoke to Christ, whom she took to be the gardener, saying, "Sir, if thou have borne him hence, tell me where thou hast laid him, and I will take him away" (John 20:15). The text implies that she had then fallen to the ground at his feet and was about to touch him. Jesus said to her, "Touch me not."

"Touch me not."

(JOHN 20:17)

If you would hear a sermon, listen to this. I cannot fathom it. "Touch me not; for I am not yet ascended to my Father: but go to my brethren, and say unto them, I ascend unto my Father, and your Father; unto my God, and your God." Magdalene was not to touch him because she did not yet believe. She thought that Christ was come again in the life in which he had been before and would so remain. Christ said there was now to be no more touching as among friends. "I do not need ointment anymore." With these words Christ said farewell to everything on earth. He had withdrawn from the land of the living, as Isaiah said (Isaiah 53:8). A partition had come between him and this world; we are divided.

But Mary was not rejected. He said to her, "Go and say unto my brethren." First he said good-bye and that he would have nothing more to do with them, and now that he would give them everything. These two sayings are absolutely contradictory. First, he would not be touched, and now he would be a brother. If we are brothers, we should be able not only to touch but to embrace. This is a strange preaching. First he tells Mary to rise and stand off, and now he calls her "dear sister." That was wonderful, and I cannot preach about it as I ought. "Go say unto my brethren." Think of what is being said. Christ is dead, buried, risen from the dead, departed from this life, without brothers and sisters, and will recognize no one. This is clear-cut. It is as if he said, "I have no one on earth," and then he speaks of brethren. There must then be a heavenly and an earthly element here bound together. He who would be a Christian, let him learn these words, "You are my brethren."

What does "brethren" mean? The disciples had all fled. They had no reason to think that they had any claim to be even servants. How overjoyed they must have been when he raised up Mary and said, "Go say unto my brethren"! That word should have raised three hundred thousand from the dead. If only they could believe it! The words are there; one has but to believe. But how? Peter had denied; the others had fallen away. How did they deserve to be called "brethren"? That means to have the same seat and right as Christ, save only that he was the firstborn among many brethren, but in the inheritance they were the same. One who is a brother is neither a lord nor a servant. There is no greater word in all Scripture this one, "Go say unto my brethren."

If the King of France or of England were to say, "You shall be my brother," and he really meant it, one would assume, "He who does anything to me is doing it to the king's brother and where the king sits and eats and rests, there, too, I may be." But no one considers who it is who speaks these words in the Gospel, for in that case, the brother would become such a lord, that no one could comprehend. For what is Christ? The greatest lordliness is in that word "brethren." If, then, we are his brothers, we are in the same inheritance and rights as he. We are not, indeed, Christ himself, but we enjoy the same privileges, and since he ascends to the Father, then, the Father and Christ and the brethren will be made, as it were, into one loaf. He who can believe that is a Christian.

Journey to Emmaus

THERE ARE TWO DIFFICULTIES in believing the account of the resurrection. The first is that the work itself is so overpowering that in this life we can never comprehend it even though faith be strong and no weakness be involved. But, as a matter of fact, there is weakness. The first difficulty God cannot mitigate. The work must and should remain as great as it is and nothing be taken from it. This is the power and the might before which all creatures, men, angels, devil, and hell must quail and fail because if this were not so, we should have to remain under our sins and the eternal wrath of God and death. But, as for the second difficulty, that we

are too weak to grasp so great a work and power in faith, God is able to look through his fingers and be patient. That is what Christ did with his disciples, who had indeed heard that he was risen, but were in such doubt that they questioned Christ himself, for they said, "We trusted that it had been he who should have redeemed Israel."

See with what care Christ gave himself to these two weak believers, how he did everything to help their weakness and strengthen their faith, because he saw and knew why they were so troubled and why they had withdrawn from the other apostles not knowing what to think or hope. The Lord would not leave them in doubt and torment but went to their aid. That was why he joined them on the way and left all the other apostles by themselves, although they also were troubled and weak enough in the faith. But because these two were in such great danger of unbelief, he suddenly joined them, as if, after his resurrection, he had nothing else whatever to do. He talked and disputed with them in such a friendly way out of the Scriptures and gave them occasion to invite him to lodge with them, to eat and to drink with them until their faith was awakened, their doubt dispelled, and they knew that he was the Christ whom they had known before and had seen crucified only three days ago but could not now recognize while on the way by reason of their doubt and weakness.

> *"As they drew nigh unto the village, whither they went: he*
> *made as though he would have gone further. But they constrained*
> *him, saying, Abide with us."*
> (LUKE 24:28-29)

That was the prayer of good folk. God permitted them to invite Christ, though they did not yet know that this was to be their salvation. Such prayer is good, but the means which we propose, God rejects. This is what happens to us; God often comes in other ways and better ways to our help.

> *"And he went in to tarry with them. . . . And he took bread,*
> *and blessed it, and brake, and gave it to them."*
> (LUKE 24:30)

The bread is the gospel and consists in this, that Christ must suffer and enter into his glory. What he had just said in words, he now made clear in a figure. He gave them the broken and consecrated bread, that is, Christ in his Passion.

"And their eyes were opened, and they knew him;
and he vanished out of their sight."
(LUKE 24:31)

Why did he vanish? When the goodness of Christ and God have been revealed and our consciences are comforted, then he goes away and leaves us hanging on the cross. Those two disciples lost his presence, but the knowledge of him they never lost again. His presence was sweet, just as his word is sweet to us, but when he vanishes, the cross takes hold, and we shudder as if he were far, far away. He does not leave his word unassailed, for after the breaking of the bread, he vanishes.

"And they rose up the same hour, and returned to Jerusalem."
(LUKE 24:33)

This means that where the gospel is not known, one cannot be silent. It is impossible that it should not be proclaimed to all men.

And being gathered with the disciples he said unto them, "Why are ye troubled? and why do thoughts arise in your hearts?" Then he not only showed the prints on his hands but asked them to give him something to eat. He had no need to do this. It was for the sake of the disciples. Previously he had had need to eat and did not wish to tempt God. He did, therefore, as a man does. So should we also. I am not under the law. My heart is free, but I can do something for the sake of another. If [the Radicals] wear gray cloaks, so also can I, not that I gain any merit by it, but for the sake of my neighbor.

"Then opened he their understanding, that they might understand the Scriptures, And said unto them, Thus it is written, and thus it behooved Christ to suffer, and to rise from the dead the third day: And that repentance and remission of sins should be preached in his name." This means that all men must be told that they are sinners. All have fallen short of the glory of God, and if one says five Pater Nosters and puts on a cowl, and his heart remains unchanged, this is no repentance. The heart must be different. The heart must be good. Repentance must come inwardly.

The article on the resurrection is the most important but the most difficult to believe. The others are hard, but this exceeds them because no article so contradicts experience as does this, for we see how men die and how bodies are mutilated. Some are devoured by wild beasts; one man leaves a leg behind in Hungary, another is burned, another drowned, and yet we are to believe that the members will be reassembled and we shall have the same bodies, the same eyes, and so on, although in an altered form. When one reflects on this, it seems as if this article were either nothing at all or, at any rate, quite uncertain. Only a few really believe it. Among the Jews only one-half believed either in the resurrection or in angels. The Sadducees did not. When reason considers this article, it simply lets it go. That is why we have to have the Scripture for it.

I have found from experience that the devil can undo me the more easily when I am not armored with the Word. He has brought me to the point where I do not know if there is a God or a Christ, and has taken from me what otherwise I know for certain. That is what happens if the heart is without the Word and faith.

The Power and the Victory

WE HAVE HEARD how the resurrection happened, and now we come to the way in which it is to be received. The resurrection should be impressed upon the whole Christian life. This is the power of faith in works. Those who faint need indeed to be told that Christ has done it all, and there is no need for us to do anything. At the same time no one is under grace who continues in sin. If you are free from sin and not subject to sin, you should not sin. Otherwise, you give proof that you are not free from sin. Justification by faith corresponds to the divine nature of Christ and good works to the human nature. They must become one person, just as in Christ divinity and humanity are conjoined.

[Then again, lest such a passage might lead to any reliance upon good works, Luther would often decry any pretention to perfection. But note how he shifts from actual sin to the sense of sin.] In 1531 he said:

In so far as you believe, you are like Christ, but at the same time feel sin and death. By faith you are one with Christ and with him you are risen from the dead. On the last day it will be manifest, but in the meantime, there is no difference between a Christian and any other man. The Christian lives in sin as does another, except that the Christian commits no gross sins, and when he falls does not stay down. Yet, a hypocrite often seems better than a true Christian. You will have to leave Christianity and sin together. In the Lord's Prayer there is the confession that we need forgiveness.

At the death of Christ the sun was darkened, but at the resurrection there were not many miracles. This may have been lest we lose ourselves in speculating night and day about the miracles and miss in so doing the true use of the resurrection. See now what Christ had done to the apostles when he died. They had supposed he would be king of the world. When, then, he died, they were desolate and felt as if they were dead themselves. Thus, God desired that the suffering of Christ should be at work in his disciples. Similarly through the resurrection the disciples were renewed and lived again. And how did that happen, if not by the resurrection? It must be powerful, inasmuch as there can be only death and affliction in the Passion. Paul says. "We are buried with him by baptism" (Romans 6:4) and "For thy sake, we are killed all the day long. We are counted as sheep for the slaughter" (Psalm 44:22). Why must we suffer such things? It is in order that we may be made conformable to Christ.

"But thanks be to God, which giveth us the victory through our Lord Jesus Christ" (I Corinthians 15:57). What does that mean? There Paul speaks of a wonderful war. This victory has come to us through Christ, and if we have the victory, we can win the war. The devil had sought to destroy Christ and had incited the Jews. They contrived by craft to take the Lord. He had done many miracles, but on the cross he was weak. Others he had helped, himself he could not help. He became a sham and they mocked his words, saying, "He has made himself to be the Son of God." Then the people turned away from him. He had predicted that he would come again. For that reason the grave was securely guarded and his enemies supposed that Christ was entirely destroyed, but then arose the goodness of God and confounded the wiles of the devil, for the Divine Majesty could not connive with all this. God summoned the devil. "Satan," said he, "you have done all the ill you could to me, but I am still alive." This is the miracle which God showed in the person of Christ. He was eternal life. Blessing and righteousness now fought against curse and death. Temporal death is now nothing against eternal life. It is as if you should try to contain the sea in a little vessel. Paul said not that Christ had overcome sin but that he had swallowed up sin (I Corinthians 15:55). Hosea said, "Death, I will be thy death" (Hosea 13:14). This is a fine word, to be the death of death. This victory is given through the gospel, as Paul said (I Corinthians 15:57). If only I believe that Christ won this victory not for himself but that we may be saved and may be lords of all creatures, not for our sakes, but for the Lord!

Just as Christ won the victory only through struggle, so also must we. If his resurrection is to work in us, we too cannot escape the struggle with death. God has permitted the old man to be at hand. The resurrection lays hold and says that whatever is of us is nothing, and I believe that when the resurrection begins to work in me, then sin and the bad conscience are dead with Christ. But from this follows that the body must die. I feel sin and death in me. The body delights in sin and fears death, and this war we must carry on so long as we live. The Lord assails us with many sufferings. Death assaults me, but I have Christ who is risen from the dead, as I also shall rise. I will hold to this. The resurrection consists not in words, but in life and power. The heart should take inward delight in this and be joyful. Outwardly, I must die as Christ died, but the gospel is a jubilant word, which the flesh hears gladly. Yet, it has no effect unless we feel it both inwardly, as well as outwardly.

Feed My Sheep

AFTER HIS RESURRECTION, Jesus appeared to his disciples and said to them, "Feed my sheep." In the Roman Church, "feed" is taken to mean the burdening of Christendom with many heavy, human laws, the selling of bishops' mantles at the highest price, the hauling in of annates from all benefices, the reservation of all foundations, the subjugation of bishops by abominable oaths, the selling of indulgences, the forbidding of the preaching of the gospel,

the plaguing of the whole world with briefs, bulls, and seals of lead and wax, the filling of sees all over the world with Romanists, and, in a word, preventing anyone from coming to the truth and living in peace.

Nobody can feed Christ's sheep unless he has love. Now tell me, if you can, whether the papacy displays such love. I am reproached as biting and vindictive, but I am troubled lest I have done too little. I ought to have taken the ravening wolves by the jaws because they constantly rend, poison, and twist the Scriptures to the corruption of the poor, miserable sheep of Christ. If I had enough love, I would have done otherwise to the pope and the Romanists who, with their laws, indulgences, and other tom-foolery, make the Word of God and faith to be of no avail.

It was to Peter that Christ said, "Feed my sheep." If this command had been given to Peter exclusively, which it was not, we should not suppose that only Peter was to feed sheep, and Paul and the other apostles were to feed mice and lice. And if it were given only to Peter, we could not assume that the pope, like Peter, should be the only one to feed *all* the sheep. The Roman congregation had the gospel for a full twenty-five years before Peter or Paul arrived in Rome, and a church is a true church no matter whether it was founded by an apostle or only by a disciple. Antioch and Alexandria were important churches alongside of Rome, and at Antioch, the disciples were first called Christians. If that had happened in Rome, the ten astronomical heavens would not be great enough to contain Roman pride. But, all churches are alike. The pope says, "I am of Peter," whereas Paul forbade these party cries. Suppose the Emperor Charles had a governor in Brabant, and this governor started out to rule also in Spain, Italy, and Germany where the emperor had appointed other governors, would that not be overstepping? I am a preacher at Wittenberg and responsible for the sheep here but not for the sheep in all the other parishes, which have their own preachers.

Moreover, the shepherd should feed the sheep without reward other than the reward of the prophets who were stoned, and that is what has happened to us at the hands of the papists. In these last twenty years many have been strangled, imprisoned, and executed with fire, water, and the sword, or driven out from land and house, from wife and child, and all on account of our feeding the sheep.

As the sun makes the day, so also does the radiance from Christ stream into all believing hearts and is at the same time in them all. As many eyes can see perfectly the rays of the sun, though there is only one sun, and as everyone has this ray perfectly, and all of them have it together, so is it also with Christ. We have him altogether and yet each has him in his own heart. When he comes he lightens and rules us all through one faith. Then the falsehood disappears and the heart rightly sees God's Word and work. There is then a new world, a new people, and a new light.

Sources

THE REFERENCES ARE to the Weimar edition of Luther's works. The citation 17,i,17.12–20.38 means volume 17, part one (which is a separate volume), page 17, line 12 to page 20, line 38. "Excerpted" means that paragraphs have been excerpted out of a section of numerous pages. "Condensed" means that sentences or phrases have been selected and blended in one or more paragraphs

The Journey to Jerusalem and Holy Week

Fire from Heaven
45,409.1–31

Peter's Confession
2,189.28–190.40

Peter and the Keys
30,ii,455.13–26

Peter and Tax Collecting
38,666.10–32

"Except Ye Become as Little Children"
37,156.18–24; 158.13–18;
159.22–160.23

"Who Is My Mother? and Who Are My Brethren?"
28,25.3–18

"Come Unto Me"
23,690.34–691.35

"Where Two or Three Are Gathered Together"
47,298.4–21

Zacchaeus
1,97.29–40

Jerusalem Beleaguered
34,ii,88.9–92.1

Mary and Martha
10,iii,269.22–270.21

Palm Sunday
10,i,2,22.21–23.8; 30.22–26;
37.32–38.25; 39.12–14

The Cleansing of the Temple
46,726.31–736.33, condensed

"Let Not Your Heart Be Troubled"
45,468.13–463.19; 470.31–471.17

"Yet Believe in God,
Believe Also in Me"
11,111.23–112.1

Temples of God
15,565.2–11

"God So Loved the World"
36,180.21–182.7
37,410.18–24; 410.29–412.16

"My Peace I Give Unto You"
11,114.2–8

"When the Comforter Comes"
10,iii,150.7–26

All Shall Bear Witness
29,341.8–19

Asking the Father
28,56.25–57.10

"I Know My Sheep"
37,73.1–11

The Lord's Supper

An Outward Sign
[1520] 6,538.35–539.5

Not an Untouchable Charm
[1522] 10,iii,70.28–71.22

Inward and Unconstrained
[1522] 10,iii,48.7–54.12

Also Outward
[1525] 18,164.31–165.3;
166.29–34; 168.15–170.25;
180.17–20

Christ's Body Not in Heaven
[1527] 23,131.7–15; 135.35–37;
139.12–140.10; 145.13–32;
150.25–32

Do Not Worry or Pry into
the Inscrutable
[1534] 37,348.16–349.19
[1519] 2,749.23–750.13

Let the Unexamined Abstain
[1523] 12,477.20

But the Timorous Are Invited
[1528] 30,i,227.5–25; 229,10–15
[1529] 29,209.1–210.16
[1534] 37,349.19–350.10

The Sacrament of Love
[1522] 10,iii,55.3–58.5

Fellowship
[1519] 2,743,7–35; 745.45–46
[1528] 30,i,26.31–37
[1519] 2,748.6–26

Arrest and Trial

On What to Meditate
41,41.10–42.18
17,i,352.21–353.7

Anointing in Bethany
46,242.19–246.10, condensed

Washing of the Disciples' Feet
29,223.8–10
46,277.9–18
29,223.16–224.5
46,287.1–7
46,295.19–297.2
20,310.28–311.2

Gethesmane
28,205.37–209.5
28,210.6–214.3
28,245.10–252.10

Trial Before Annas and
Peter's Denial
28,258.5–261.7
28,268.8–273.4
28,279.2–289.8

Trial Before Pilate
28,298–393, excerpted

The Crucifixion
28,385.10–393
34,1,250
29,244.16–247.12
37,355.21–32
17,1,67–84, excerpted
2,136–141
1,337.10–344.10, excerpted

The Resurrection

The Empty Tomb
29,258.19–259.24
32,49.29–52.2, excerpted
29,259.7–277.9, excerpted

In the Garden
27,116.5–10
29,294.9–297.4, excerpted
29,292.2–301.5, excerpted

Journey to Emmaus
21,255.17–226.19
15,528.29–529.24
20,349.11–350.18
28,429.22–431.14
32,58.18–22

The Power and the Victory
27,124.31–125.8
34,i,275.13–276.3
15,517.23–519.20

Feed My Sheep
6,306.20–34
6,319.12–320.21–33
54,275.3–278.8
9,669.10–18